D0433066

for **Placing Siblings**

Hedi Argent

Published by
**British Association for Adoption & Fostering
(BAAF)**
Saffron House
6–10 Kirby Street
London EC1N 8TS
www.baaf.org.uk

Charity registration 275689 (England and Wales)
and SC039337 (Scotland)

British Library Cataloguing in Publication Data
A catalogue record for this book is available from the British Library

ISBN 978 1 905664 33 7

Project management by Jo Francis, BAAF
Designed by Andrew Haig & Associates
Typeset by Fravashi Aga
Printed in Great Britain by T J International Ltd
Trade distribution by Turnaround Publisher Services, Unit 3,
Olympia Trading Estate, Coburg Road, London N22 6TZ

BAAF is the leading UK-wide membership organisation for all those
concerned with adoption, fostering and child care issues.

The paper used for the text pages of this book is FSC certified.
FSC (The Forest Stewardship Council) is an international network
to promote responsible management of the world's forests.

Printed on totally chlorine-free paper.

FSC
Mixed Sources
Product group from well-managed
forests and other controlled sources

Cert no. SGS-COC-2482
www.fsc.org
© 1996 Forest Stewardship Council

Contents

Introduction   1

Tip 1: Allow children to say who their brothers
and sisters are   6

Tip 2: Know the policy and guidance   15

Tip 3: Keep siblings together; help siblings
to part   22

Tip 4: Know the child; know the sibling group   30

Tip 5: Make kinship care for siblings the
first choice   38

Tip 6: Recruit and prepare families for each
sibling group   46

Tip 7: Devise strategies to help unrelated children
to become sisters and brothers   54

Tip 8: Support siblings and families after
placement   63

Tip 9: Ensure that parted siblings can share
their lives   75

Tip 10: Mark the difference: a checklist for
working with siblings   84

Endpiece: Sally Poskett   88

Useful organisations   93

Note about the author

Hedi Argent is an independent family placement consultant, trainer and freelance writer. She is the author of *Find me a Family* (Souvenir Press, 1984), *Whatever Happened to Adam?* (BAAF, 1998), *Related by Adoption* (BAAF, 2004), *One of the Family* (BAAF, 2005), *Ten Top Tips for Placing Children in Families* (BAAF, 2006) and *Josh and Jaz have Three Mums* (BAAF, 2007). She is the co-author of *Taking Extra Care* (BAAF, 1997, with Ailee Kerrane) and *Dealing with Disruption* (BAAF, 2006, with Jeffrey Coleman), and the editor of *Keeping the Doors Open* (BAAF, 1988), *See You Soon* (BAAF, 1995), *Staying Connected* (BAAF, 2002), and *Models of Adoption Support* (BAAF, 2003). She has also written five illustrated booklets in the children's series published by BAAF: *What Happens in Court?* (2003, with Mary Lane), *What is Contact?* (2004), *What is a Disability?* (2004), *Life Story Work* (2005, with Shaila Shah) and *Kinship Care* (2007).

This series

Ten Top Tips for Placing Siblings is the fourth title in BAAF's *Ten Top Tip* series. This series tackles some fundamental issues in the area of adoption and fostering with the aim of presenting them in a quick reference format. Previous titles are *Ten Top Tips for Placing Children*, *Ten Top Tips for Managing Contact* and *Ten Top Tips for Finding Families*.

The next title to be published in the series will be *Ten Top Tips for Preparing Careleavers*.

Acknowledgements

I wish to thank Erica Amende, Sarah Borthwick, Mo O'Reilly, Alan Rushton and Phillida Sawbridge for their helpful comments on earlier drafts of this book. I am grateful to Shaila Shah, Director of Publications at BAAF, for her everlasting support, and to her assistant Jo Francis for her never-failing helpfulness in taking this book to print. My most heartfelt thanks go to the children and families who have taught me what I know about placing siblings.

Introduction

> **Practitioners who want to take sibling issues seriously, face a challenge of comprehension and comprehensiveness even before they begin.**
>
> (Mullender, 1999, p 322)

Sisters and brothers have always provided rich material for literature. Siblings offer endless opportunities for stories of rivalry, loyalty, opposites, envy and enduring love. The story of Cain and Abel has the gravest warning about sibling rivalry and is closely followed in the Old Testament by the sorry tale of Jacob, who tricked his older brother, Esau, out of his birthright. Shakespeare used brothers and sisters in his plays to compare the good and evil sides of human nature: Edgar and Edmund, Goneril, Regan and Cordelia in *King Lear*, Antonio and Prospero in *The Tempest*, Frederick and the Duke in *As You Like It*. But he also celebrates the strength of the sibling bond: Isabella is ready to sacrifice her honour to save her brother in *Measure for Measure* and Viola and Sebastian rejoice in their magical reunion at the end of *Twelfth Night*. And Shakespeare doesn't overlook or undervalue the tie between unrelated children who are brought up together. Celia and Rosalind in *As You Like It* choose to face a dangerous future together in preference to being parted, and Helena's speech in *A Midsummer Night's Dream* is a testament to good substitute family care.

> *Helena (Act 3, scene 2):*
> *We, Hermia, like two artificial gods,*
> *Have with our needles created both one flower,*
> *Both on one sampler, sitting on one cushion,*
> *Both warbling of one song, both in one key,*
> *As if our hands, our sides, voices and minds*
> *Had been incorporate. So we grew together,*
> *Like to a double cherry, seeming parted,*
> *Two lovely berries moulded on one stem.*

Many writers, like Dostoyevsky in *The Brothers Karamazov* and the authors of the *Mahabharata*, have used siblings to point out different attitudes to a common problem, while George Eliot and Jane Austen, and more recently Chimamanda Ngozi Adichie in *Half of a Yellow Sun*, have given us some of the most tender descriptions of sibling relationships in adversity. Children used to grow up with tales of Hansel and Gretel, Jack and Jill, and with family adventures by Enid Blyton, Arthur Ransome, E Nesbitt and CS Lewis – all good moral fun with large rival groups of altogether jolly siblings. Nowadays, of course, they are more likely to read about Harry Potter, who has a nasty foster brother, or to watch television and to come across the darker side of family life. Certainly none of us will remain untouched by cultural or personal experiences or prejudices when we approach sibling issues.

Like other books in the Ten Top Tips series, this one is neither an academic study nor a comprehensive manual. It is a summary and a reminder of what is involved when we consider siblings in foster care and adoption. These considerations go far beyond whether sisters and brothers should be placed together or apart. The tips that follow offer practical suggestions about work with genetically related and unrelated siblings in many different situations and circumstances.

The term "sibling" is not defined in law. Childcare legislation urges us to keep siblings together whenever possible but doesn't tell us who siblings are: does the word describe half-sisters and half-brothers and stepsisters and stepbrothers? Are "real" siblings only the ones who share at least one parent, or are they also the children who grow up together in a shared family setting? The endpiece in this book tells the story of a family with 15 children: three were born to the parents, six came in three sibling groups and the rest joined the family one by one, not necessarily in chronological order; all of them became brothers and sisters. Some were close, some teased and annoyed each other; most showed affection and concern and tried to help each other; the younger learned from the older; and they all learned how to handle conflict according to their individual characters and temperaments.

Children have fewer full biological siblings now than they did 100 years ago, but more diverse family structures are creating more complex sibling relationships. It is often difficult for social workers to have an overview of "who is who" in a family and "who belongs where". In a study published in 1996, Marjut Kosonen found that social workers were unaware of the existence of one-third of the siblings of the children on their caseloads. If either or both of a child's parents have already had children with previous partners, and then separate and start another family, if they lose children to adoption or if they are placed in foster care, how can we evaluate the importance of the extended sibling network? Perhaps the best people to help us are the children themselves, if we can work with them as partners and experts in their own lives, as Tip 1 suggests.

There can be no doubt that sibling relationships are significant. It is self-evident that they are potentially the most long-lasting. After about the age of five, more interaction goes on between children than between parents and children. Children learn who they are by comparing themselves to important others, and siblings play a critical role in this process, which usually continues into adulthood.

Adult adoptees search for siblings as often as for parents. Younger sisters and brothers who have been separated in the care system call helplines to find each other. A 12-year-old boy in foster care was asked who was most important to him; he said it was the postman. When asked why, he said: 'Because he brings me letters from my brother'. It would seem, therefore, that separating children from each other is as serious a step as separating them from their parents. Tip 2 examines the policy behind decisions regarding siblings, and Tip 3 explores the rewards and risks of placing siblings together or apart.

The words "sisters and brothers" have different cultural meanings. Some languages emphasise the importance of sibling relationships: in Urdu and Hindi, siblings are addressed by the words for brother or sister rather than by their names. In some religions, everyone is hailed as a sister or a brother; in the Hawaiian tradition, all members of the same generation are called "brothers and sisters" no matter what their relationship, and many African-Caribbean communities do not differentiate between half, step and full biological siblings. We have to be careful not to rely on a purely Western interpretation of sibling connections when we make placement decisions. Tip 4 looks in detail at how not only cultural differences and ethnicity, but also attachment styles, developmental trauma and disability can affect individual children and how they relate to each other.

Relationships between sisters and brothers who have endured a variety of negative experiences together are likely to be different from other sibling relationships. A common history of adversity does not automatically lead to a sibling bond; it may result in maladaptive behaviour and severe attachment difficulties. Children may need to make a secure attachment to an adult before they can relate in any real sense to another child. Emotional recovery may be impeded if siblings keep reminding each other of their traumatic past, but they may also find comfort and consolation because they have survived as a family unit. The most important factor for recovery must be the new carers' input and commitment to the sibling group alongside their relationship with each child; family and friends have a head start because they already know all the children. Tip 5 addresses the special circumstance of kinship care for siblings.

Research studies have described the outcomes of sibling placements, and raised the issue of other children in the family, but there has not been a systematic enquiry into which types of professional practice influence sibling placements to work or to disrupt. What preparations do siblings and prospective siblings and their families need? What should family placement workers be doing when they plan for sibling groups, or when they place children in families that already have birth or adopted or foster children? Tips 6 and 8 explore the recruitment and support of families who want to care for more than one child, and Tip 7 offers guidance for direct work with all the variations of sibling groups found in foster care and adoptive placements.

Social workers have to struggle with the parallel principles of acting in every child's best interests and of keeping brothers and sisters together. This is often a conflicting task. We cannot guarantee permanence to any child or sibling group. We can only strive to provide stability and we have a duty to maintain continuity for all children who have to leave their birth parents. Sisters and brothers can offer lifelong continuity to each other; even if they cannot live together, good contact arrangements between separated brothers and sisters can enable them to share at least part of their lives. Tip 9 discusses the ways and means of doing this.

The most valuable contribution to this book has been made by the sisters and brothers I have been privileged to work with and by their families. The last tip is a reminder and a summary of all I have learned from them. The names and details in personal communications and case studies have been changed to preserve anonymity without compromising the relevance of the material.

Hedi Argent
June 2008

Further reading

Adichie CN (2007) *Half of a Yellow Sun*, London: Harper Perennial

Kosonen M (1996) 'Maintaining sibling relationships: neglected dimensions in child care practice', *British Journal of Social Work*, 26, pp 809–22

Mullender A (ed) (1999) *We are Family: Sibling relationships in placement and beyond*, London: BAAF

Wedge P and Mantle G (1991) *Sibling Groups in Social Work: A study of children referred for permanent family placement*, Aldershot: Avebury

TIP 1

Allow children to say who their brothers and sisters are

> *We must strive to lift (each other) as we climb. We must strive in such a way as to guarantee that all our sisters, regardless of social class, and indeed all our brothers, climb with us.*
>
> *(Davies, 1989, p 158)*

This was Angela Davies proclaiming the political sense of sisterhood and brotherhood at the height of the Black Power movement in the US. She was using a form of language rooted in African community tradition and reinforced by many religions. It says to the world, 'All the people like us are our brothers and sisters and we stand or fall together'. It is not likely that children will make this kind of statement when asked who their brothers and sisters are, but we may be surprised to hear from them about complex family structures and relationships that are not all recorded on social work files.

We know that at least 80 per cent of children who become looked after have siblings. They may be in the same placement, with other foster or adoptive carers, at home with both birth parents or split up between former partners; they could be living with relatives or friends; some may be grown up and living independently. Any of these sisters and brothers could seem to be closely connected or quite indifferent to each other. And they are only the ones who are in some way genetically related! When we add the unrelated stepsiblings, the birth children in foster and adoptive families, and the other unrelated fostered and adopted children in the same family, we have a very rich heritage indeed. A heritage we must regard as a treasure for the children we work with, although it can easily become an administrative conundrum when social workers are hard pressed to find permanent family placements while maintaining meaningful connections between siblings.

Meaningful connections

Shane and Sandra, aged eight and six, were placed together in what was hoped to be permanent foster care. This was their third move in two years. They had been in separate foster homes for a year-and-a-half before adopters who could take both children, and could maintain contact with the birth family, were found. This placement disrupted after six months because Shane injured the older birth daughter of the family, for which the prospective adopters blamed the frequent contact arrangements with his own siblings. They wanted to keep Sandra, but it was decided that the children should not be separated again and that permanent foster care would more easily enable them to stay in touch with their birth family.

Two older brothers were adopted as infants by different families and are now 10 and 12 years old; both have letterbox contact with their birth family. Two older half-sisters live with their maternal grandmother and have a caring relationship with Shane and Sandra. A younger brother and sister were born when the mother married an older man who has been a steadying influence and has helped her to stop misusing drugs. Each sibling pair has a different father. Shane and Sandra's father has had three more children with a new partner; he has always stayed in touch with Shane and Sandra. Sandra was very close to the daughter of the prospective adopters; Shane misses a child of his own age who was fostered with him. They were nicknamed "the terrible twins".

How can we enable children to hold on to such a very extended family and to make sense of their sibling relationships? Clearly, Shane and Sandra cannot keep up regular visits with 11 sisters and brothers who live with different people in seven different places. The children's social worker wanted to be fair to all the related siblings and devised contact arrangements that gave equal weight to their relationships and enabled them to come together in different combinations. This involved the most complicated organisation and use of resources and resulted in an inflexible, unsatisfying experience for the children and an exhausting one for the families. Sandra asked her foster carer, 'Whose turn is it to see me next week?'

When a new social worker took over, she saw that she had to unravel the situation. She began by working separately with Shane and Sandra to find out who their most significant brothers and sisters were. She devised pictorial representations of the sibling network.

> *Sandra chose to have a sibling bouquet of flowers. She and Shane were the only large dark red blooms held together in the middle, her two older sisters and the prospective adopter's daughter were smaller and paler and sticking out a little further; her mother's and her father's young children were tiny pink buds around the edge of the bouquet and her adopted brothers were tall, indistinct and fern-like, decorating the bouquet but set apart from the flowers.*
>
> *Shane decided to put his siblings in rings around the moon. He was the moon all by himself. In the ring closest to him he placed Sandra and his "twin" foster brother. In the next ring, he put all his half-siblings except his adopted brothers. He said they couldn't go in a ring around the moon, but they could have a star all to themselves.*

Next, the new social worker agreed a contact plan with the children and their families: a plan to reflect Shane and Sandra's feelings, to be practical enough to sustain in the long term and flexible enough to adjust to changing circumstances. After all, even in the most well regulated large families, it is improbable that all brothers and sisters will have stable, equal relationships throughout their childhood. Some will leave home while others are still at school; as adults, some will see each other often, some hardly at all – most will, at least, keep each other in mind.

Only children

But what about the lone child separated from parents? Peter has no genetic siblings. He was placed in foster care as an infant and, after

9

four more moves, to an adoptive placement when he was three. His strongest attachment was to the last foster carer's son, but no one talked to him about having to leave the boy he called 'my brother'. Peter's adoptive parents were amazed at the strength of his feelings. A one-off meeting, three months after placement, reinforced Peter's sense of loss:

> *He constantly wants to look through his life story work and bombards us daily with questions about the foster carer's son. He doesn't understand why he has disappeared again. We really feel for Peter who is clearly struggling to make sense of his world with the vocabulary and understanding of a three-year-old.*
>
> *(James, 2006, p 99)*

Should we explain to a young child, like Peter, that his brother is not really his brother? And even if we can help him to understand the genetic model of brotherhood, is that more important than the emotional bond? Possibly Peter's "brother", another only child, had an equally unhappy time. One boy of eight told his mother's supervising social worker: 'I help with her and that, she's like my own little sister, when she goes I'll cry and cry if I don't see her no more.' We usually try to avoid making the distinction between "real" and "unreal" parents in adoption and foster care, yet we often rob children of "unreal" siblings because we don't hear what they tell us, or what they can only tell us by their behaviour.

Shared childhood or shared heritage?

> *Arnold and Elly enjoyed a mutually supportive brother–sister relationship until Elly died when she was 94. As unrelated children, they had lived in the*

same foster home for 15 years, where they had been treated with rough kindness from birth to adolescence. Neither had any knowledge of their origins, but together, in their words, they were "two against the world". When they had their own families, their children and grandchildren mingled in and out with each other, as cousins do, but their own relationship remained central throughout their lives. In their old age they decided to trace their birth families. Elly discovered three living half-sisters; she was delighted to find out where she belonged; she met them and liked them and left it at that. Arnold found a deceased half-brother, whom he could not mourn.

There is no doubt that Elly and Arnold, when they were children, would have told us unequivocally who their sibling was. As adults, their shared childhood in foster care proved to be far more significant than their unshared genetic heritage. Yet that shared childhood was experienced differently by each of them – Elly fondly remembered small kindnesses while Arnold still smarted from the unjust blows – a reminder that all children have different experiences in the same home with the same parents or carers.

In contrast to Elly and Arnold, who became siblings in foster care, are the many siblings who are separated in infancy and yearn for sisters and brothers they didn't know, or barely knew and cannot remember. For them, the blood tie is paramount; they seek someone who resembles them and who can fill a great gap in their lives. So we must never assume either that a shared childhood is more important than a shared genetic heritage. In fact, it is never safe to assume anything about sibling relationships, which is why we should always start by listening to the children.

The lost baby

Children who are in foster care or are adopted often show a great interest in a new baby sister or brother at home with their birth mother. Will the baby be safe? Does she look like me? Will she ever know I'm her brother? Why can't we adopt her too? Mixed in with curiosity and concern is probably a renewed feeling of resentment about his own separation from his birth family. Why me and not her? When asked, he might put the new baby on top of his list of siblings and be telling us, in his own way, that he is in a muddle about his sibling relationships. If the muddle is not resolved, it could lead to more confusion and problems in the future.

David, aged five, was adopted by a single parent. She was very keen to maintain contact with his two younger sisters (the second, a baby, born after David was placed) who were adopted, one at a time, by a couple in the same county, and with two older brothers placed separately in foster homes. David enjoyed seeing his older brothers but went frantic after every visit to the other adopters. He became violent towards his own adoptive mother, had nightmares and was excluded from school. Only after skilled therapeutic work with David was it discovered that he believed his baby sister had been kidnapped and that he wanted his adoptive mother to rescue her.

Hate can be as meaningful as love

Even siblings who torment each other whenever they are together, who apparently have nothing in common and who have been separated to protect one from the other, may have a strong sense of brotherhood. Joe's older brother ignored him, and his other brother couldn't speak to him because he had an impairment; contact meetings were not happy occasions. Yet Joe pleaded with his adoptive parents to take his brothers too.

Joe talked a lot about his "before people", especially his two brothers who were now placed with another adoptive family. And although social workers and foster carers considered his relationship with them to be of little significance because he constantly fought with them, even hurt them, we knew it was very significant. Possibly equal to his feelings for his parents. He gradually adjusted to having no "day-to-day brothers" as he called them, and accepted that he could still love them even if they lived elsewhere. But once he was putting a video of them into his special wooden box, when he said, 'They're in a coffin now'. When I asked, did he know what a coffin was used for, he replied, 'It's for dead people'.

He was six years old at the time, and it taught me never to underestimate children.

(Royce and Royce, 2008, pp 31–32)

Joe was lucky to have parents who listened and maintained a connection that would have been easy to write off as "undermining the placement".

Points to consider

- Children will tell us which sisters and brothers they are connected to.
- Children may not wish to differentiate between full, half, foster, step or adoptive siblings or to talk about "real" and "unreal" sisters and brothers.
- Not all sibling relationships have equal weight and value for a child; in most families there are alliances and pairings, but the children who fight most might also feel closest to each other.
- There are many different cultural, religious and political views of

sisterhood and brotherhood.

- Single children, especially, may make important attachments to children who are not related to them.
- Babies born after children are separated from their birth mother may have a special significance for the separated child.
- There is more danger that children will lose their paternal than their maternal half-siblings.
- It is not uncommon for siblings to search for each other 60 years after separation, when their adoptive parents have died.
- There is no evidence to show whether a shared childhood or a shared genetic heritage is of greater importance. It all depends on the children and on the circumstances.

> *I've got a brother that's, like, always been my brother and a sister what's adopted like me. I know I've got another brother – I see him sometimes and I like it when I see him. Then there's them two other girls – I forget about them 'cause we never see them, but I want to.*
>
> *(Alan, aged seven)*

Further reading

Davies A (1989) *Women, Culture and Politics*, New York: Random House

James M (2006) *An Adoption Diary*, London: BAAF

Mullender A (ed) (1999) *We are Family: Sibling relationships in placement and beyond*, London: BAAF

Royce R and Royce E (2008) *Together in Time*, London: BAAF

TIP 2

Know the policy and guidance

> *If it is acknowledged that local authority services should aim to place siblings together, then a range of support services need to be in place. Similarly, when there are concerns about the viability of maintaining siblings within a single placement, a clear assessment should always inform the placement plan.*
>
> *(Beckett, 1999, p 114)*

In 1999, when Shelagh Beckett conducted her study of social work policy regarding siblings, 10 out of 16 local authorities said they did not have a written statement. Only three agencies had comprehensive guidance; one had two lines in its procedures manual, which advised that siblings should be placed together 'unless it is part of a well thought out plan based on the children's needs' (Beckett, 1999). It is to be hoped that a similar study today would produce more reassuring results, but we cannot afford to be complacent. Careful assessments of whether children should be placed together or apart require added resources and place greater demands on social workers. Departmental policy can make or mar the placement of sibling groups.

The official guidance is quite simple: the local authority should, if practicable and consistent with each child's welfare, ensure that siblings who have to be accommodated, are placed together. But what is practicable and what is consistent with each child's welfare?

Children in sibling groups do not arrive as a surprise. It is to be expected that most children who have to be "looked after" will have brothers and sisters of one kind or another. Even if they don't enter the care system together, the chances are that one will follow another. Every local authority needs to have a clear mechanism for planning for children in sibling groups from the beginning of the care process.

The most commonly given reason for separating siblings is that no family could be found to take three, four or more children, and it is therefore deemed not to be practicable to place them together. The second most common reason is that the siblings have different needs, and it is therefore not consistent with each child's welfare to place them together. What is the strategy for recruiting families for sibling groups? And how are the children's relationships and needs assessed? Tips 4 and 5 go into more detail about assessment and recruitment, but the policy to support good practice has to be in place first.

Points to consider

- Are workers trained to undertake direct work with children and to understand the dynamics of sibling groups and relationships?
- Do adoption and permanency panels have sufficient training and advice regarding sibling placements?
- Are there mechanisms in place for making assessments and decisions about keeping siblings together or separating them, or uniting or reuniting them in permanent placements? Regular departmental "sibling" meetings for social workers and their managers can offer a forum to discuss the sibling groups on their caseloads.
- Is there an approved list of consultants, including medical and educational advisers, who are available and affordable to assist in making decisions regarding sibling placements? Having to start

from scratch, case by case, can be discouraging for overloaded social workers.

- Is there support and supervision for working with sibling groups, including recognition of the extra demands on time? Assessments can only be as thorough as time allows.
- What is the policy if the children in a sibling group do not share the same ethnic heritage? It is not enough to say that permanent carers should reflect and promote the children's ethnicity.

One social worker did his best to "match" a sister and brother who had the same Irish mother and different fathers from Iran and Nigeria. The children were separated because a match could not be found and it was thought, although there was no clear policy, that the "black" child should be placed with a black family and the "white" child with a white family.

- Is there a direct route to funding for families who require and qualify for help with housing, transport and equipment in order to care for a sibling group?
- Is there clear guidance for involving siblings, according to age and understanding, in decisions to keep them together or apart?
- Is there a format for recording decisions about sibling placements that will give the correct information and explanation to brothers and sisters in the future?
- What is the policy about staying in touch if siblings have to be separated: are resources, including mediation, available to facilitate meaningful contact arrangements? And is there guidance about what might constitute meaningful contact?
- Is there a clearly stated preference for placing siblings with family and friends? The percentage of children placed in kinship care varies wildly between agencies because the pursuit of kinship placements seems often to be left largely to the commitment of individual workers.

- The decision to separate siblings is sometimes justified by having to make realistic care plans for the courts. Is there departmental guidance about persuading the courts that there are people wanting and able to take several children if adequate support packages are offered?
- Are prospective permanent carers of siblings entitled to read the children's files? If not, how is all the information conveyed?
- Are post-placement support plans for siblings and their families agreed, monitored and reviewed? Is the agency Adoption Support Services Adviser/post-placement support worker clearly identified?
- Is the policy regarding sibling placements circulated and discussed in team meetings?

Supportive agency practice for siblings

Family Group Conferences have become established practice for some agencies, but not for all. Based on the belief that the children's network has the greatest understanding of its own strengths and weaknesses, Family Group Conferences enable family and friends to come together to explore their own resources and to make decisions in the best interests of children. Most birth relatives are intensely concerned about splitting up siblings and may come up with solutions to keep them together in the family, which have not been previously considered.

The Family Rights Group (see *Useful organisations*) has developed a particular style of Family Group Conference which is not managed by social workers and is set up by an independent co-ordinator. But there is no hard and fast rule about how kinship networks should be involved in making plans. Any model that allows extended families to be heard is good for children. Sometimes conferences can be held on smaller scales or at different stages. If a decision is made to split a sibling group, a family conference is a good way to discuss the reasons for the separation, and the implications for the children and the birth family members in the future.

A **Child Appreciation Day**, or **Presentation Day** as it is sometimes called, is recommended for all placements but should be considered essential for a sibling group. It is hard enough to get to know all there is to know about one child, let alone a group of several children. There is no better way for sharing a great deal of information in a relatively short time than to give over a whole day for prospective permanent carers to meet all the people who can contribute to an understanding of the siblings. It is a small investment compared to the cost of a disruption due to incomplete or misunderstood information. This is an opportunity for seeing and hearing a multi-faceted view of each child illustrated by videos, photos, anecdotes and facts, and of getting an impression of the impact the siblings have made on previous carers. The agency's legal, medical and educational advisers should be available for at least part of the day to clarify matters regarding the children's health, schooling and status in order to avoid misunderstandings and misinterpretations. Social workers can produce visual aids on flip charts: flow diagrams, family trees and circles to represent moves, losses, separations and relationships can sometimes communicate more than words. Such a day should be regarded as a guided tour through the children's lives: as one adoptive mother said, 'It gave us the chance to put the questions we didn't know we wanted to ask'. Some agencies invite an independent chairperson to manage the meeting, but a more informal structure usually works well, and a shared lunch is a good foundation for working together.

Activity Days or **Adoption Parties** are possible ways of linking families with sibling groups. They give families the opportunity to respond directly to children, and perhaps to make a connection which social workers might have missed. Children can enjoy the events as special treats and a chance to have a good look at the variety of families who want to be permanent carers. Adoption Parties for brothers and sisters waiting for families, and approved families who may be able to take siblings, are perhaps particularly suitable because every child will feel relaxed and secure in their own familiar group.

Activity Days are more structured than Adoption Parties and based on group preparation and support of children, current and prospective families and social workers. Families are linked to the specific children they have expressed an interest in following publicity; they spend a day keeping them occupied, safe and fed, and at the end of the day they can talk to the social workers and current carers with more confidence. Preparation of siblings and families, leading to matching and placement, can then focus on the needs and abilities of real people.

Other models along these lines could be developed by agencies working together to find more families for children who are "hard to place", and that includes most sibling groups. It is cost-effective if several children find families as a result. The process can be energising for workers, fun for children and empowering for carers and prospective families.

Extended Family Preparation Meetings during the home study phase are useful tools for helping prospective carers to include their network in their plans and to assess how much support they will have. It also allows social workers to share information, outline procedures and answer queries. To become related to an older child by adoption or permanent foster care is not an everyday experience; to become the uncle, aunt, cousin or grandparent of more than one child, all at once, is quite an adventure!

> *Three large children coming into the family, just like that, it took some getting used to. We didn't know how to work it with the other grandchildren and some of the other relatives never got around to it really. It would have helped if we'd been more part of it but my daughter was always that stressed before they came, and after, she never stopped.*
>
> *(Adoptive grandmother of sibling group)*

Corporate values

Policy to support social workers in their dealings with sibling groups has far-reaching long-term consequences. The value put on sibling relationships will determine the level of effort made to keep sisters and brothers together. In the absence of a clear policy and corporate responsibility to plan for siblings, outcomes are dependent on the values and commitment of individual social workers – and this serves the best interests of neither siblings nor agencies.

> *The task of planning for children in public care is an onerous and complex one, which is fraught with difficulties. In order to plan effectively, it is crucial that departments recognise the particular needs of siblings and take steps to address them.*
>
> *(Beckett, 1999, p 126)*

Further reading

Argent H (2004) *Related by Adoption*, London: BAAF

Beckett S (1999) 'Local authority planning and decision-making for looked after siblings', in Mullender A (ed) *We are Family: Sibling relationships in placement and beyond*, London: BAAF

Department of Education and Skills (2005) *Adoption Agency Regulations* 2005, London: HMSO

Family Rights Group publishes a range of information on Family Group Conferences (see *Useful organisations*)

Lord J (2008) *The Adoption Process in England*, London: BAAF

TIP 3

Keep siblings together; help siblings to part

In an ideal world, one would have looked to all three children being placed together and that didn't work because grandparents were only able to take Paul and not the other two, and I don't think adopters would have taken Paul because of his difficult behaviour.

(Social worker quoted in Ellison, 1999, p 130)

Many of us bring our own strong feelings about keeping brothers and sisters together to our family placement work with siblings. But there are equally strong warnings about the implications of allowing sibling relationships to overshadow every child's primary need for attachment to a parent figure (see *Family Futures Assessment Handbook* (Burnett *et al*, 2008)). So which do we put first in the hierarchy of needs: the prospective parent–child relationship or the existing child–child bond? Evidence is scarce, but is slightly weighted towards keeping sisters and brothers together. Research by Rushton *et al* (2001) found that families with a single placed child were more likely to report a difficult first year; the seminal study of long-term placements undertaken by Fratter *et al* (1991) found that, when siblings were placed together, the outcomes were marginally better. Hegar's overview of 17 relevant studies found that:

> *Sibling placements are as stable, or more stable, than placements of single children or separated siblings, and several studies suggest that children do as well or better when placed with their brothers and sisters.*
>
> *(2005, p 731)*

However, we do not know about the quality of assessments leading to decisions to place siblings together or apart, nor do we know whether children who are placed singly were perhaps older and had more difficulties than the siblings who stayed together.

Placement considerations

All together now?

If several children are to be placed together, should they be placed at the same time or one at a time? There is something to be said for "serial" placements that follow the more usual model of building a family; very large sibling groups might join a family in pairs, like twins. It gives time for initial attachments to be established, and for more preparation, especially if children who have been separated are to be reunited. It may offer the opportunity to build or rebuild relationships gradually, without the tensions of day-to-day living; but it also sets the scene for natural jealousy and resentment of the newcomer mixed with existing sibling rivalry. It would be essential, therefore, if using such a model, to involve all the siblings from the beginning so that they understand, according to age and ability, the aims and purpose of the whole process.

> *One local authority had found a family to take five*
> *siblings aged between four and 11. All the children*
> *were introduced to the new family, shown where*
> *they would live and even where they would sleep.*
> *They were included in the planning sessions and*
> *agreed that the oldest should move in first 'so that*
> *she would be able to help the others to settle*
> *because she would know her way around'. The*
> *remaining siblings made frequent visits to their new*
> *home, and helped to get their rooms ready until the*
> *middle two moved in together. The two youngest*
> *joined them six weeks later after several overnight*
> *stays. They all felt part of their special placement*
> *project.*

Alternate pairs

When large sibling groups have to be split up, it has been reported by carers that pairs of sisters and brothers, who are not next to each other in age, are easier to manage (Lord and Borthwick, 2008). Obviously, this cannot be approached in an arbitrary manner, and must also be closely connected to the reasons for splitting the children up in the first place.

Diverse heritage

Brothers and sisters frequently do not share the same ethnic background. Either or both of their parents may have had different partners and produced children with diverse dual heritages. A choice might have to be made about matching an ethnically diverse sibling group with permanent carers; each child's need for an ethnic link will have to be balanced against all other needs, including staying with their brothers and sisters. Family systems reflect class and community values as well as ethnicity and religion – it would not be possible for families and their adopted children to share every attribute. It would be more desirable to find families which can deal with diversity than to separate siblings according to colour, religion or culture. A half-brother and sister, one white, one black, brought up by a single parent, said: 'It's good. We're both special and we're together.'

Disability

Sometimes it is tempting to separate a disabled child from his siblings because he has clearly defined special needs. It may indeed be necessary to place him on his own for a variety of reasons, but disability should not be the only reason. All children have special needs, and their attachments, behaviour, roles and place in the family may be at least as important as their abilities or disabilities. It could be that separation produces feelings of shame for the disabled child and lifelong feelings of guilt in his siblings for relinquishing him.

Sexual abuse

They want to get away from their past and make new lives for themselves. This doesn't mean they don't know where they came from. But if you come from hell, wanting to experience a bit of heaven before you look back isn't too unreasonable, is it?

(Smith, 1995, p 97)

Respite from siblings who share a history of abuse may be the only way to promote healing, and to enable each of them to make a secure attachment to an adult. But the need for respite can easily lead to permanent separation and exacerbate feelings of blame and exclusion. We have to make flexible plans to meet changing circumstances, to accommodate the healing process but also to validate the children's experience by allowing them to bear witness. Unsabotaged contact while they are parted and regular reviews of progress are essential, whether reunification is the aim or not.

If siblings have abused each other, they will require therapeutic help before any decisions can be made about keeping them together in a permanent placement. Prospective carers should have detailed information about the abuse rather than a general indication that it has taken place.

> *An older, childless couple was told that the girl of 10 and boy of 12 they wanted to adopt had been subjected to 'inappropriate sexual activity with strangers and each other in a paedophile ring'. They didn't know what that meant exactly and didn't like to ask. A week after the children were placed, they were horrified to find them apparently having full intercourse. Only then was therapy offered for the children and counselling for the adopters. The placement held because the couple were empowered to deal with the behaviour and the children wanted to normalise their relationship. But the situation could easily have spiralled into hysteria and permanent separation, which would not have tackled the problem, and would have caused both children deep grief.*

Reuniting siblings

Reunion may have to be balanced against the risks of uprooting some children from other secure settings. For instance, it may be thought that a newborn baby has no existing relationship with a teenage sister who has been settled in foster care for several years, but this should not mean that the connection is ignored.

If children who have lived separately might be reunited in a permanent placement, much preparation will be needed for each child and the whole group together. They will have to revisit their shared experiences and understand their shared heritage; they will have to become familiar with each other's separate lives; they will have to build or rebuild their relationships; and they will have to learn about living together again with a new family.

It can be helpful to devise a pictorial model of siblings' parallel and divided lives and their progress towards becoming a new family. Trains changing track, boats diverging when the sea gets rough and coming together in calmer waters, footsteps in the sand, climbing a mountain from different starting points, or simply large scale maps can offer opportunities for discussion while enjoying an activity together. It should become clearer during this work whether or not children are ready to be reunited, and what the difficulties for them and their new family might be. If a large sibling group is to be reunited, it might be easier for the children and the family if one or two of the siblings move in one at a time, as suggested earlier.

Roles

Every child in every family assumes a role or has a role assigned to them. It is, of course, important to consider how children see themselves and are seen by their sisters and brothers; two roles in particular have to be taken into account when family placement decisions for siblings are made – the scapegoat and the child-carer.

We are inclined to think it is wrong for the older child in a sibling group to take responsibility for her younger brothers and sisters; we sometimes feel the older child should be given the chance of childhood by being separated from her siblings. This is a typically Western view that may or may not fit a specific scenario. In some other cultures, there is a notion of respect for older siblings together with an expectation that the older will look after the younger; the idea of responsibility in childhood is not regarded as a risk to healthy development and "parentified" older siblings are the norm. So we must tread more softly – a child's self-esteem may be built on her caring capability; the most secure attachments of younger children may be to their older sister, and it could be more appropriate to work with a family to accommodate and gently influence their unusual relationship than to separate the children.

The scapegoated child is another matter. The phrase "preferential rejection" describes what happens to a child who is always the one to be blamed, left out, pushed aside, ignored, neglected, picked on and singled out for abuse of all kinds. If the "scapegoat's" brothers and sisters are part of this deadly game, the child may need to be rescued from siblings as well as parents. Only a careful assessment will tell if relationship patterns might change, or at least be modified, in a supportive permanent family.

Children's wishes

It may be that children themselves express a wish to be placed on their own (one boy of nine declared: 'I'm not one of us'), that they ask to be "paired" with a particular brother, or that a group rejects one sibling. Usually some direct work with each child and with the whole group will clarify what is going on; it may then become possible to place them together or it could be wise to keep them apart. It is always unwise to make hasty assessments of sibling relationships in short-term foster care. Sisters and brothers who have been uprooted may take their unhappiness out on each other because they feel too helpless to do anything else. Foster carers need to be encouraged to nurture the sibling connection rather than be expected to judge whether siblings should be placed together or apart.

> *One adoptive family described how their three older children had initially not wanted to be placed with their younger brother. When life story work was done, it transpired that, when the children were all at home, this child had been taken out by the mother while the other three were abused by their stepfather. When this was explored and talked through with the children, they could accept that this different treatment was beyond the control of them all and the older three became much less antagonistic towards their brother and they were eventually all placed together.*
>
> *(Lord and Borthwick, 2008)*

Questions and answers

The questions about parting siblings or keeping them together are complex – there are no clear answers and some contradictions. It is never enough to state that children have strong bonds or different needs as reasons for parting them or keeping them together: strong bonds could be devastatingly destructive, and all children have different needs. Factors that could lead to separation may also point to keeping children together. There is no substitute for assessing each case separately, no matter what similarities they have to another.

Further reading

Burnell A, Vaughan J and Williams L (2008) *Family Futures Assessment Handbook*, London: Family Futures Publications

Ellison M (1999) 'Planning for sibling continuity within permanency', in Mullender A (ed) *We are Family: Sibling relationships in placement and beyond*, London: BAAF

Fratter J, Rowe J, Sapsford D and Thoburn J (1991) *Permanent Family Placement: A decade of experience*, London: BAAF

Hegar R (2005) 'Sibling placements in foster care and adoption: an overview of international research', *Children and Youth Services Review*, 27:7, pp 717–739

Lord J and Borthwick S (new edn. 2008) *Together or Apart?*, London: BAAF

Macaskill C (1991) *Adopting or Fostering a Sexually Abused Child*, London: Batsford

Rushton A, Dance C, Quinton D and Mayes D (2001) *Siblings in Late Permanent Placements*, London: BAAF

Smith G (1995) 'Do children have the right to leave their past behind them?', in Argent H (ed) *See you Soon*, London: BAAF

Thoburn J and Rowe J (1988) 'A snapshot of permanent family placement', *Adoption and Fostering*, 12:3, pp 29–34

TIP 4

Know the child; know the sibling group

> *Tim, aged six, asked by his teacher to complete a written sentence starting with 'I am good at...',*
> *writes in a bold hand: 'I am good AT BEING ME'*
>
> *(Cairns, 2002, p 10)*

If only all children were as sure of who they are as Tim was. Unfortunately, most of the children who need family placements are likely to have had distressing experiences that have affected them both as individuals and as members of their sibling group. If their infant needs for nurture and safety have been neglected, they will most probably have a distorted understanding of the world, a confused sense of identity, low self-esteem, and troubled relationships with their siblings. It is a fallacy that children who suffer adversity together will necessarily forge strong bonds. They may, but they are as likely to scrap like puppies over a bone if that is all they are used to getting.

And furthermore, each child in a sibling group will respond differently to the same circumstances: one child may feel favoured and loved because she is first in line for her father's sexual attentions, while her abused sister feels despised and victimised by her father, and the other members of the sibling group will react according to gender, age and their own unique experience in the family.

Factors influencing sibling relationships in the birth family

- The quality of each child's early individual attachments to the primary carer: secure, ambivalent/avoidant, disorganised. 'I remember that when I was a child I had wonderings and feelings that came from a place so deep inside me that I never could have put them in words even if I wanted to'. (Oaklander, 1978, p 320)
- The quality of the parental relationship: conflictual, violent, co-operative. Are any of the children involved in domestic violence, taking sides or protecting a parent?
- The social climate in the family: anti-authority, isolated, open. Do children feel the world is with them or do they have to stand together against the world?
- The emotional exchange in the family: blame, shame and punishment, praise and reward. Are there "good" and "bad" children in the sibling group?
- The impact of trauma on each child: damage to the developing brain, impulse, stress and anger regulation. 'Trauma hits hardest at those who are most vulnerable, but the overwhelming terror experienced can cause even the most securely founded and resilient person to disintegrate' (Cairns, 2002, p 99).
- The role each child plays in the family: baby, spoilsport, joker, tell-tale, spokesperson, ringleader, tomboy, daredevil, bookworm, genius, dunce, goodie, little madam, real boy, peacemaker, victim, bully, and so on. One adoptive mother said: 'We were left with this little clown who thought he was safe as long as we laughed, and with his brother who had to prove he was in charge every minute of the day.'
- The family's material resources: housing, food, clothes, bedding, toys. Have the children any sense of ownership?
- The family structure: different fathers/mothers, ethnicities, religions,

significant relatives. Does a grandparent have a caring relationship with one, some or all of the children in a sibling group?

● The family's values: attitude to skin colour, gender, disability, work, money, substance misuse. One girl said: 'I'm nearly white and my sister's nearly black'. A boy of five asked his social worker to 'Buy me a bit of hugs'. A slightly older boy believed that it was 'OK to use drugs if you like having the needle'.

It is notoriously difficult for adults to walk in children's shoes. The most painstaking observations may not reveal the subtle interactions, beliefs, fears and narratives that form the basis of sibling relationships. How can we ever learn to understand their private language? Perhaps the best we can do is to watch, to listen, and to hear the silence and the behaviour behind the words. Even then, perhaps in the end only the fairly obvious is measurable. Nevertheless, in order to work with brothers and sisters we not only have to find ways to assess how they relate to each other, but we also have to understand the dynamics of the sibling group and the needs of each individual child.

Points to consider

● How does the group deal with stress in the family, how do the siblings deal with conflict within the group, how does each individual child react to pressure?

● Do siblings recognise each other's distress and support and comfort each other, do they close ranks against outsiders?

● If individual children get pushed out because they have hurt or upset brothers and sisters, are they able to rejoin the group?

● Does any one child take responsibility, or blame, for the actions of all?

● Can each child express feelings and wishes, or is there a spokesperson?

● Who initiates play? Is play boisterous and pleasurable or competitive and aggressive?

● Which children "gang up", "pair off" and which appear to be "loners"?

● How and to whom do individual children show affection?

● Who irritates, teases or tries to get others into trouble?

● Who shares secrets, interests, or copies each other's behaviour?

- Do children assume distinguishable roles? How do siblings describe each other?
- How does each child rank in the sibling group and gain the attention of adults?

In *Together or Apart* (2008), Lord and Borthwick reproduce sibling relationship checklists that were originally included in *Patterns and Outcomes in Child Placement* (Department of Health, 1991). These are useful tools for assessing sibling pairs, but do not consider the dynamics of larger groups. The Strengths and Difficulties Questionnaire (SDQ) (Goodman, 1997) is also helpful when assessing individual children within a sibling group.

Expert opinions and substance misuse

Each child in a sibling group will have a medical report that will deal with individual health matters and, if thought necessary, assessments from a psychiatrist and/or psychologist. There is, however, a danger that, when children from the same family are affected by parental substance misuse, as so many are, not enough attention is paid to the different degree of damage each child may suffer. The scale of the problem is immense, with some local authorities reporting that 60–70 per cent of the young children they are placing for adoption have been exposed to alcohol and/or drugs *in utero*.

Affected children may have physical manifestations including the distinct facial features of foetal alcohol syndrome, cerebral palsy and sight impediments, but the majority may have no physical symptoms, and yet be even more vulnerable and have equally, and possibly more challenging, long-term problems. Many have learning disabilities and, as they become more aware that some of their behaviours are not normal, they become depressed and their self-esteem suffers. Within the non-functioning parts of their brains, they lack the skills to link actions with consequences.

Unfortunately, it is not uncommon for the signs and symptoms of Foetal Alcohol Spectrum Disorder (FASD) to be misunderstood. Based on international medical studies, it is estimated that 1 in 100 children are affected by FASD. That equals 6,000–7,000 children born in the UK each year. It is also estimated that at least 90 per cent of children who have Alcohol Related Brain Damage are not being diagnosed, and therefore there is no specific help and advice for the affected children who are placed with substitute families.

David was placed with Wendy and her husband Ian when he was two years old. He had a history of neglect, lack of stimulation, little speech and he was unable to play. He had attention-seeking behaviour and abnormal attachment patterns – he would spit when frustrated.

His sister, Charlene, followed him into the placement later when she was 18 months old. No investigation had been done into the effects of the large quantity of alcohol their mother had drunk during pregnancy. Because the children's health and behaviour improved dramatically when they were removed from their mother, it was thought that all they needed was the right permanent family.

David thinks he's ugly and boring, knows he's different but doesn't know why and – if asked why he has done something naughty – he says he has to do it! He is bright, but, like his sister, finds it hard to make friends. At school, David had difficulty with concepts like telling the time, comprehension and maths. He could not understand numbers and, although he learned to read, he could not remember the stories or answer questions about them. He was always losing things and refused to do any homework. His IQ was on the lower end of the normal range and therefore his school teachers could not understand why they would explain something to him one day which he would understand and repeat back to them, but completely forget the next day. They assumed he was being disobedient and would scold him accordingly.

When Charlene was placed, she was described by Wendy as 'a little scrap with tufts of hair and too small to be registered on the centile scale'. She had to have speech therapy from quite early on in the placement. When she started school, she did not engage with any of the other children. At seven, she was constantly on the move and showed no sign of recognising danger.

Life became chaotic – the children could not understand why they needed to get up for school, could not manage the washing and dressing routine, and would never hurry. It took more than five years for the correct diagnosis to be made.

With hindsight, Wendy and Ian feel that if they had had accurate and full medical information before the children were placed, they would have been able to understand the children's behaviour, get more training for themselves and generally be better parents to their children. Knowing that children cannot make sense of instructions means that you can address the problem in a different way. As Wendy put it, if you don't know your child has Foetal Alcohol Syndrome, 'Parenting is like trying to get around Seattle with a map of San Francisco'.

(Communication from Parents for Children) *

* Parents for Children (PfC), an adoption and fostering agency based in London, has an action research project to assess affected children who are looked after by local authorities in England and Wales. The project has a multi-disciplinary team which assesses the needs of each child and advises on a programme of treatment and support. PfC then recruits permanent families for the children and offers long-term support both to the children and the family. A multi-disciplinary review is built in to the programme (from information supplied by Parents for Children).

No short cuts to "learn" the child

It makes huge demands on social workers to work with each child separately as well as assessing them as part of a sibling group. But there are no short cuts to getting to know a child. If we miss the opportunity to know each child, we will not be able to tell prospective carers who that child really is, and families are built with children, not with groups. Misleading or inadequate information about one child can lead to the placement disruption of a whole sibling group or to the removal of that one child from the group.

> *Looking back, they told us lots about the other two, but very little about Janice. We realise now, it's because they didn't know her, not because they didn't want to tell us.*
>
> *(Adopter at disruption meeting)*

Core assessments and permanence plans for each child are a statutory requirement, but the quality will depend on knowing the child. Individual life story work is essential to maintain the minutiae of children's personal histories and to validate their own rather than their sibling identity. Being able to compare how sisters and brothers recall and respond to a similar set of circumstances, and how they want to present themselves, can be very enlightening for prospective carers. The adopter at the disruption meeting above knew Janice only in relation to her younger disabled sisters who had a raft of special needs; they had no notion of how Janice struggled to get away from being the able, caring sister, to becoming a troubled 10-year-old in her own right.

It has been shown that core assessments are often not as fully completed for black and minority ethnic children as for white children. Whether due to lack of expertise, or to difficulty in gathering information across language and cultural divides, this calls for specialist guidance and advice and should not be allowed to result in information gaps.

The more information that prospective carers are given to "learn each child", the better will they be able to welcome each real child into the family.

> *Do you know who you are? You are unique. In all the world there is no other child exactly like you. In the millions of years that have passed, there has never been a child like you.*
>
> *(From a Jewish prayer to welcome a new child into the community)*

Further reading

Argent H (2006) *Ten Top Tips for Placing Children in Permanent Families*, London: BAAF

Cairns K (2002) *Attachment, Trauma and Resilience*, London: BAAF

Department of Health (1991) *Patterns and Outcomes in Child Placement*, London: HMSO

Department of Health (2000) *Framework for the Assessment of Children in Need and their Families*, London: The Stationery Office

Goodman R (1997) 'The Strengths and Difficulties Questionnaire: a research note', *Journal of Child Psychology and Psychiatry*, 38, pp 581–586

Howe D (ed) (1996) *Attachment and Loss in Child and Family Social Work*, Aldershot: Avebury

Lord L and Borthwick S (new edn. 2008) *Together or Apart: Assessing brothers and sisters for permanent placement*, London: BAAF

Mullender A (ed) (1999) *We are Family: Sibling relationships in placement and beyond*, London: BAAF

Oaklander V (1978) *Windows to our Children: Gestalt therapy approach to children and adolescents*, Boulder, CO: Real People Press

Thomas C and Beckford V with Lowe N and Murch M (1999) *Adopted Children Speaking*, London: BAAF

TIP 5

Make kinship care for siblings the first choice

I am 61 and my wife is 49. We have had our grandchildren with us for 16 weeks; it's been very hard work for us both. The effect of how they were being treated is beginning to come out now – the effect that drugs are having on this generation – I feel it's just the tip of a very large iceberg. I have had to give up a job, so no income at all as yet. We have applied for all we can get but as yet nothing.

(Grandparent quoted in Grandparents Plus Newsletter 5)

Families and friends who look after children – kinship carers – do not get a very good deal. Inconsistent and uneven services throughout the UK mean that some potential kinship carers do not trust children's services. If they foster, they do not always get all the training, support and special allowances that non-kin foster carers get; if they don't want to become foster carers, they may get only minimal financial and social work support, or none at all. Many kinship carers are unaware of their rights, their options and their legal position. It is not surprising then if they are prepared to take one child but balk at the thought of taking another. Sibling groups are often split because one child has been taken in by a grandparent or other relative at a time of crisis, while sisters and brothers go into stranger foster care.

> *Carrie's daughter, Jade, had profound learning difficulties. When she was 16, she had a relationship with an older man and had a child. Carrie had no hesitation in taking on the permanent care of the baby while helping Jade to remain as involved as possible. Two years later, Jade moved out of the family home and immediately became pregnant again. The local authority approached Carrie about taking the second child. Carrie now has both children but she is adamant that she cannot take any more. She has residence orders and allowances far below the fostering level; she is finding it hard to pay for childcare so that she can keep her job; she has no other support, although Jade has started drinking heavily and is often drunk when she visits.*

If kinship care for siblings is to be seriously pursued as the most desirable option – and we have a duty to consider placement with family and friends as the first choice for every child – then we have to look to our policy and practice to see whether we can offer a package that makes it more viable. We have to start by acknowledging that many kinship carers may be older and have health problems, that they may be less well off, have less space in their homes, and be less assertive than other permanent carers. And we must remember that they have not applied to become substitute parents – they are stepping in to keep children in the family. They mostly offer care because they love the children and are able to build on existing relationships; they may be motivated by loyalty to a relative or friend or by the need to rescue children from chaos; very occasionally they may be driven by an unforgiving sense of duty or the desire to get even. We would do well to devise a different set of measures when we assess kinship carers; meeting the National Minimum Fostering Standards may not meet the needs of children, or support their kinship carers. That does not mean we should lower our standards of care, but it does mean that we should widen our views of what good care might be.

Points to consider

- Does the agency culture promote kinship placements as the first choice for sibling groups? Are social workers encouraged and supported to explore kinship care as the best option?
- Can we guarantee kinship carers a fostering-related, non-means-tested income per child?
- Is there at least one named and experienced kinship care worker in the agency?
- Is there an information pack specifically designed for kinship carers in all local community languages that spells out all the options available, including residence and special guardianship orders?
- Is there an assumption that families from minority ethnic groups prefer to manage kinship care without outside help and support? Or is it recognised that they need support as much as other families do, but may have more difficulty in accessing it?
- Does the agency offer a specially designed training and assessment procedure for kinship carers?
- Is there a payment and support package for kinship carers who do not want to foster and prefer to have an informal arrangement? Fostering is not a comfortable fit in all kinship care situations.

An older woman, who had looked after her two grandchildren for six years, reluctantly became their foster carer in order to qualify for the financial

> *support she increasingly needed as they reached*
> *their teens. She was horrified when faced with a*
> *diary she was expected to fill in daily, with forms to*
> *complete for statutory reviews and with obligatory*
> *training days four times a year.*

- Is legal advice easily available for kinship carers who want to apply for a residence or special guardianship order? And is there sufficient provision for financial and post-placement support for kinship carers who choose one of these routes?
- Is there an accepted process whereby kinship carers who take a sibling group can be given financial help with housing and transport needs?

Issues for siblings in kinship care

Who is who?

Kinship placements change relationships. A doting granny or an indulgent uncle can become strict parent figures; a young aunt may suddenly turn into an older sister, and cousins may seem to be additional siblings. If babies are permanently placed with kin, they may grow up confused about who their parents are and who is who. If brothers and sisters remain together in kinship care, they may have different notions about family relationships according to age and personal experience: one sibling may have a greater prior attachment to the caring relative and resent the intrusion of the others; if there is hostility between parents and carers, children may be exploited to take opposing sides to reflect the alliances in the family or the split between the maternal and paternal relatives. It can be hard for siblings to remain loyal to parents, to carers and to each other if the adults around them cannot co-operate or if they compete for the children's affections. If siblings are split up between family members and friends, or if one or more stay with the parents, there is likely to be envy of whichever child or children appear to be having the better time.

It is clearly essential to prepare kinship carers for the potential relationship tensions. It can be helpful to sort out right from the beginning: what will the children call the carers? How can each child hear and tell the same kinship story? Can children be protected from family feuds? How can the sibling relationships be preserved and enhanced?

Siblings bringing up siblings

Maria was a single-parent refugee with five children. Her husband, who had been a dissident under a repressive regime, had "disappeared". Maria worked as a home help for the local authority and did office cleaning some nights. One day she just dropped dead, leaving an 18-year-old student daughter, Agnes, and four school-aged children, aged between eight and 14, living in a council flat in a tower block. The local authority acted swiftly. They found two foster placements for the younger children and offered Agnes a place in a student hostel. Agnes was horrified. In her culture this was unheard of. She would not allow the loss of their parents to be compounded by further separations. She insisted that she could look after her sisters and brothers while she continued her studies. A sympathetic social worker guided Agnes through the legal tangles of becoming her siblings' legal guardian, and provided the family with a peripatetic childcare worker, adequate allowances and the tenancy of their home.

It would have been easy for a less confident young woman to lose control and for the children to become permanently separated. Even if

Agnes had not been of an age to take formal responsibility for her siblings, a carer might have been found to move in with the children to prevent family break-up.

Managing contact arrangements

If contact between children and their parents and other family members can be left to everyone's good will, and if the children feel happy about it, then there is no problem. But contact can't always be as flexible as one might want it to be. It may be circumscribed by court orders (or children's hearing orders in Scotland) if parents or other relatives are thought to pose a threat to the children or to the security of the placement. One child could be asking for more contact than the kinship carer thinks wise and another could be refusing to have any contact at all in order to punish a parent. If brothers and sisters see parents and other relatives at different times and more or less often, this can give rise to new feelings of rejection or superiority, to bullying and scapegoating. That is not to say that siblings should always visit or be visited as a group – far from it, but the arrangements should be open and made with every child's knowledge and understanding. One grandparent discussed the next week's contact arrangements with her three granddaughters every Sunday evening while they made the sandwiches for their school lunch.

If there is conflict in the family about a kinship placement, then contact can become too fraught to sustain, especially when several children are involved, without professional help to manage, support, monitor and review the arrangements.

> *Of the advantages that kinship care offers, promoting good long-term quality links with the children's mother and father must be one of the greatest; but it is here too that the complexity can be at its greatest.*
>
> (Pitcher, 2002, p 55)

Managing money

Grandparents Plus, the Grandparents' Association and the Family Rights Group (FRG) are inundated with stories of hardship from kinship carers. Even when they claim all they are entitled to, like the grandfather at the beginning of this chapter, they may have to wait for weeks or months before any payments are made. Family crises are not planned, and even if they are anticipated, very few relatives and friends have the ready means to look after a sibling group without immediate financial help. When this help has not been forthcoming, kinship carers have had to raise mortgages, cash in pensions and annuities, take out high-interest loans, sell precious belongings, and use up all their savings.

In the long term, relatives and friends who care permanently for several siblings may have to move house and buy a larger car; they may have to give up work or change jobs to fit in with their childcare responsibilities; or they might have to relinquish all hope of a comfortable retirement. The difference between expenses for an older couple and for a couple looking after a group of growing children is astonishing. It is not really cheaper, as they say, to feed two than one, and three ravenous youngsters eat ten times more in a day than two people with diminishing appetites. Best not to ask what three pairs of trainers can cost.

> *If they [kinship carers] are acceptable caretakers, then they should not be denied ongoing financial support – such denial only serves to punish the children.*
>
> (Geen, 2003, p 2)

Although kinship carers who foster must be paid the same basic allowance as non-kin foster carers, it would be hard to believe that any relative or friend takes on a sibling group for the money. There are easier ways to make a profit. The fact that kinship carers will need at least as much financial help as strangers, and perhaps more, should never be a barrier to keeping siblings in the family.

The final say

> *My gran, she's 100 per cent, she's been our rock and kept the whole family together. If it wasn't for her we'd probably all be separated and not grown up with each other...I wouldn't be the stable person I am today if it wasn't for my gran.*
>
> *(Quoted in Broad, 2001, p 20)*

Further reading

For adults

Argent H (2005) *One of the Family: A handbook for kinship carers,* London: BAAF

Broad B (ed) (2001) *Kinship Care: The placement choice for children and young people*, Lyme Regis: Russell House Publishing

Broad B (2005) *Relative Benefits: Placing children in kinship care*, London: BAAF

Broad B, Hayes R and Rushforth C (2001) *Kith and Kin: Kinship care for vulnerable young people*, London: National Children's Bureau

Geen R (2003) 'Finding permanent homes for foster children: issues raised in kinship care', in Geen (ed) *Kinship Care: Making the most of a valuable resource*, Washington DC: UI Press

Grandparents Plus newsletters published quarterly (see *Useful organisations*)

Pitcher D (2002) 'Is Mummy coming today? Managing contact arrangements in kinship placements', in Argent H (ed) *Staying Connected*, London: BAAF

For children

Argent H (2007) *Kinship Care: What it is and what it means*, London: BAAF

TIP 6

Recruit and prepare families for each sibling group

> *They needed a family, they needed to stay together, and we'd always wanted two. But when we saw the three of them on the TV, it was like it was meant for us.*
>
> *(Adopter of three siblings under five)*

If applicants are interested in adopting or permanently fostering a sibling group, they are likely to have a specific number of related children in mind.

But children who need to be placed with their sisters and brothers come in several times as many "varieties" as single children do, and it is even more impossible to prepare for them without knowing them. If a prospective carer or adopter imagines that they could look after two children, they might in fact stretch to three or even four if they are encouraged to respond to children who need a family, rather than being approached about sibling groups of the correct size. It is perhaps more realistic to devise a specific recruitment campaign for each group of three or more siblings and to work with the families who come forward. Much good publicity comes free if the confidentiality issues can be agreed: local radio stations and newspapers are always keen on "human interest stories". With luck, one family will emerge that goes on to be the right family.

If more than one family stays the course, they may wait in the wings until another sibling group needs them. Current trends, confirmed by data from the Adoption Register, suggest that larger sibling groups are among the most difficult children to place.

Points to consider

- We have to be clear why children should be placed together and believe that they can be placed together. We have to be equally clear about why siblings should be separated.
- Approved families should not necessarily be given preference: training, assessing and preparing a family for the complexities of a specific group of children may produce sounder placements.
- It is not enough to say that children 'need a black or dual heritage family' or that 'we are looking for a family that can promote and reflect the children's ethnicity and culture', especially if sisters and brothers do not share both parents. Other publicity has to be devised; links with faith groups and with communities have to be explored and cultivated (Rule, 2006) to encourage people of diverse and mixed ethnicities to come forward. Members of minority ethnic groups should know that a high value is placed on what they have to offer.
- Most people who take more than two children will require financial help with housing, transport, equipment, childcare, possibly education, and almost definitely, therapeutic support. Given the histories of most children we place, it is likely that at least one, if not all of, the members of a sibling group will need

therapy of some kind, and many placements have floundered while families waited for funding from their local authority. What could be available, and how needs will be assessed, should be clearly spelt out in the recruitment material. It must be a financially daunting prospect, for all but a few families, to even consider taking several children at once.

- Single people seem to be able to manage surprisingly large sibling groups. Might there also be an alternative model? Could a close network of single carers become the sibling group's parents?

- If the greatest need of a large sibling group is to stay together, and if it seems impossible to place them all with one family, then perhaps the recruitment process could be turned on its head. A housing association or local authority might provide the children with their own home, and find a family to place with them instead. This model has been successfully tried and tested for at least one sibling group of five ranging in age from four to 15, and for three disabled, unrelated children of 10, 11, and 12 who had grown up together as siblings in a residential home.

- It is always advisable to discuss the possibility of more children being born to the same parents. Permanent carers need to know where they stand: would they be expected to take another child, or would they be given first choice?

The Khans, a couple in their late forties, adopted four brothers and sisters aged between four and nine. The children were very dependent on each other, but gradually bonded with their new parents. The two older ones had a hereditary learning disability. The whole family had regular counselling from a post-adoption service. After three years, the children's birth mother had a new baby who was immediately accommodated and later freed for adoption. The birth mother wanted the baby to join his siblings. The Khans applied but were turned down because they had 'more than enough on our plate already'. They appealed. They said that the

> *baby would "cement" their family and give the other children a common focus. The post-adoption agency supported them. The baby was placed with the Khans; the parents were able to help their other children to experience the infant nurturing they had missed, by sharing in their brother's care. All five children thrived; the parents were exhausted but survived to feel that they had made the right decision.*

What was right for the Jacksons could well have been wrong for another family. It is our job to enable families to explore what they can and cannot do, rather than to weed them out in order to meet our expectations and stipulations. Preconditions, such as "there should be no other children in the family", "these children need a two-parent family" or "their special needs indicate that they should be placed separately" may put off the very family that would be the right one for siblings.

> *Margaret read about two severely autistic deaf brothers, aged six and eight, who, it was said, needed to be placed separately, each in a two-parent family, because they had to be closely supervised and physically restrained. It happened that Margaret was a teacher at a school for deaf children, and had brought up her own autistic son. She now lived alone in a large house in a supportive community. She felt strongly that these two brothers should stay together, and persuaded their local authority that she could manage if given enough support. With the help of generous grants and a rota of paid and volunteer helpers, she*

> *managed very well. She adopted both boys, and organised their move to fully supported independent housing when they were in their early twenties.*
>
> *(Argent, 2006, p 29)*

If a large sibling group is to be split up only because it is thought that no one can take so many children, then that ought to be plainly stated in the recruitment material. There just might be someone out there who says 'I'll take them all if you help me'.

● Prospective carers may have a range of motivations for wanting to foster or to adopt a sibling group: they may have tried for many years to have their own children and now want the family they might, by now, have had; they may be older and have brought up one set of children and relish the thought of starting again – but not quite at the beginning; they may come from large families and are close to their own brothers and sisters or they never had siblings and do not want to replicate that pattern. They could have strong feelings about keeping siblings together, or they may be attracted to a specific sibling group.

● "Danger signals" may include permanent carers hoping it will be easier to take more than one child because they expect the children to be company for each other or for their birth children, or if adopters persuade themselves that they want older siblings because they are desperate for the baby that comes with them.

What prospective carers need

Even if families have been approved before they apply for a specific sibling group, the most important part of the placement process will be the preparation for having these particular children. Agencies have their own procedures for working with families, but it is vital never to curtail that part of the work that deals with *this* family's preparation for *these* children. It is helpful to think of this stage as "linking" a sibling group with a family and to delay the formal "matching" until the compatibility of the children and family has been assessed and the family's commitment confirmed (Cousins, 2003).

- All permanent carers need all the available information about every child, and that goes for each child in a sibling group. People who are entrusted with the responsibility of caring for a group of children must be entitled to know all there is to know about each child. Information should never be censored, and it should be supplemented in any possible way wherever there are gaps. Ideally, prospective carers should have access to the children's files and the opportunity to discuss the implications of what they have read with social workers, medical and educational advisers. In interagency placements, it is essential that the family's worker has read the files before a link is made.

- Families will need guidance to decide what is confidential and what can be shared with others. Children have a right to privacy: not every detail of their stories has to be told to all friends and neighbours, or even to all relatives. Teachers and doctors may have to know more for professional reasons.

- If children have been physically or sexually abused, safeguarding them and other children in the family will have to be thoroughly discussed. The exact nature of the abuse of each child should be described: the age, gender and identity of the perpetrator, the child's age during the period of abuse and the frequency of it; how the child was groomed, whether the child was threatened or bribed to keep it a secret, and whether the child was heard, and by whom. Even siblings living together will not all have had exactly the same experiences of abuse, and it will be important for carers to be aware of what each child knows and understands about it so that they are aware of the "triggers" that can re-activate the trauma. All families who foster or adopt a sibling group in which one or more of the children has been abused should be offered expert counselling even before the children are placed.

Five-year-old Carl, placed with his two older sisters, had a tantrum every time anyone produced a camera. His adoptive parents said that the tantrums were more like episodes of terror. They knew that

> *the children's parents had taken Carl to have his*
> *picture taken for pornographic websites while his*
> *sisters were made to watch. They were able to*
> *explain to teachers, friends and relatives that the*
> *children were "camera shy" and should not be*
> *persuaded to have their photos taken.*

- Prospective carers need to know exactly how far each child in a sibling group has been affected by substance misuse, inherited disabilities, environmental factors and early relationships. Some training in attachment theory is helpful for all permanent carers: when siblings are being placed, prospective parents need to understand each child's attachment patterns, and to accept that each child will adjust at different rates and evoke different feelings in the carers.

- People who apply to adopt a sibling group are proposing to introduce several children at once into their immediate and extended family. Preparation for birth children must be taken very seriously indeed and is dealt with in a subsequent chapter in this book.

- The quality of preparation for a sibling group will depend on how well each child is known to the social workers and how far the prospective permanent carers can engage with the necessity of considering each child as an individual; it will also depend on the social workers' and the family's understanding of the sibling group dynamics and the impact of that group on the carers and their family system.

- During this intensive preparation, families may discover that they cannot, after all, become the parents of this sibling group; or workers may have to decide that this family is not right for these children. It ought to be clear that every stage offers the choice of proceeding or calling a halt; but it should also be clear that families who cannot become parents to one sibling group may be the right parents for another, or they may be better suited to adopt one child at a time.

In the end, we cannot fully prepare a family for any child, let alone for a group of children. Numerous carers have said that nothing could have prepared them for the reality of living with their children. We can only try to give families the tools to understand what is happening and the support to hang on.

> *To begin with we were stunned. It was like being on a treadmill morning, noon and night. We were prepared for all their behaviour and squabbling and the bedwetting and being scared and getting upset, but we just couldn't have imagined how tired we would be. And the noise level deafened us after being on our own for so long. And we didn't know how sad they would make us feel about losing their parents. We thought we'd be just fine, but we went on for a long time needing all the support we could get.*
>
> *(Adoptive parent of three children under five)*

Further reading

Argent H (1998) *Whatever Happened to Adam?* London: BAAF

Argent H (2006) *Ten Top Tips for Placing Children in Permanent Families*, London: BAAF

Cousins J (2003) 'Are we missing the match? Rethinking adopter assessments and child profiling', *Adoption & Fostering*, 27:4, pp 7–18

Rule G (2006) *Recruiting Black and Minority Ethnic Adopters and Foster Carers*, London: BAAF

TIP 7

Devise strategies to enable unrelated children to become sisters and brothers

The Video

When Laura was born, Ceri watched.
They all gathered around Mum's bed –
Dad and the midwife and Mum's sister
and Ceri. 'Move over a bit', Dad said –
he was trying to focus the camcorder
on Mum's legs and the baby's head.

After she had a little sister,
and Mum had gone back to being thin,
and was twice as busy, Ceri played
the video again and again.

> *She watched Laura come out, and then,*
> *in reverse, she made her go back in.*
>
> *Fleur Adcock*
>
> *(With kind permission of the author and Bloodaxe Books (Astley (ed), 2002)*

All children have mixed feelings when the anticipated arrival of a new baby is announced, and the reality of this new little person often doesn't live up to expectations. Children have to learn a hard lesson when they discover that they have to share their parents, their space and their belongings. When their initial curiosity has been satisfied, and the excitement has given way to not getting the attention they have been used to, many an older child has asked their mother to take the baby back to the shop.

If established sibling groups have to make room for one more, they may compete with each other to become the new child's special sister or brother, or they may band together to keep the upstart out. The larger the sibling group, the more diluted the impact of one more.

Whatever the family structure, however many children, and whichever culture they adhere to, most biological siblings share lifelong relationships that may range from intimate and loving to distant and resentful. But how are sibling relationships formed and affected when children are added to the family not by birth but by adoption or permanent foster care?

Points to consider

- Most children profiled in family-finding magazines and newsletters are well past infancy and have had negative experiences quite unlike any that the children who are to become their new siblings have known. They will certainly have accumulated many losses along the way if they have been separated from parents, friends and relations, including their full, half, step or foster sisters and brothers. If they join a new family, it will not be the same for the birth children as their mother having another baby, any more than adoption is the same as giving birth.

- If siblings are going to be placed together, they may bring their own united front or troubled interactions with them. It can be very hard for birth children to welcome siblings with a pre-existing relationship into their home. Sometimes it is easier if brothers and sisters are placed one by one, in order to mimic the biological way of building a family.

- When older children are placed on their own, they may transfer familiar patterns of sibling behaviour to their new sisters and brothers. It can be distressing for birth children to become embroiled in behaviour that they cannot understand, especially if this includes sexually inappropriate behaviour.

A girl who had been consistently bullied by her much older brothers, and therefore separated from them, provoked her older adoptive brother until he lashed out, so that she could go on playing the victim.

Another girl, who had been praised by her father for spying on her older sisters, told tales about her new sister because it was the only way she knew of gaining favour from adults.

A boy of only five, who had played sexual games with his sister, distressed the teenage daughter in his adoptive family by trying to fondle her breasts whenever she wanted to give him a cuddle.

- Biological parents and their children have several months to get ready for the birth of the next child, which is regarded as a natural family event. Adoption and foster care are considered as somewhat different, and it is generally accepted that good training and preparation for permanent carers are the cornerstones of good placements. Prospective adoptive and foster siblings, relative to their age and understanding, need as much preparation and support as their parents do.

- Birth children should be included in at least some of the training and home study sessions. A special Saturday morning event for children whose families are in the process of becoming permanent carers can set the scene for later peer support activities. And parents should be encouraged to share and discuss the adoption plan with their children even before they make an application.

> *We'd talked to the other children [birth children aged 15, 13 and 11] before that first phone call. We were always clear we could not go ahead without their support. We'd talked in general terms about children who needed families, and engendered some excitement and enthusiasm...We kept stressing that it might not happen; that we might decide not to go ahead; that we might not be approved and so on. But a momentum developed after that first phone call that led to William [aged four] joining our family a few months later.*
>
> (Marsden, 2008, p 19)

Not only the preparation, but also the seven-year age gap between William and Robbie, the youngest birth child, probably contributed to the success of this placement. Neither William nor Robbie saw each other as rivals. Robbie could finally achieve the role of older brother, while William could at last become the indulged baby in a family.

- Some parents understandably hope that the nearer children are in age, the closer they will become. But children who have not had enough love, attention, food or protection are rarely ready to share, to be loyal or to give and take; they may not even know how to play or understand what is theirs and what belongs to another child. They may need to feel secure in the placement and to trust the adults before they can relate appropriately to their own age group. It can cause pain to birth children if their overtures are repeatedly rejected.

- If a disabled child, who may need permanent care, is fostered or adopted, the existing siblings, when old enough, need to know that they will not become responsible for an adult disabled sister or brother unless they choose to. Many children who foster or adopt do become carers themselves when they grow up, not because it is expected of them, but because it is a way of life they have learned to value.

- If unrelated children are sequentially adopted or permanently fostered, they also have to be helped to become siblings. They will have the added difficulties of unshared problematic backgrounds and relationships and different contact arrangements, as well as their individual genetic inheritance. They may find it more threatening than birth children to accept a stranger into the family because their security has been harder won and has to be more jealously guarded.

> *It has taken time for our boys to attach to each other. I am not suggesting that they have a healthy strong relationship, but they are certainly not indifferent to each other. Starting from a month-long honeymoon, which quickly sank into mutual loathing, they somehow grew to respect each other; loyalty developed and a bond, albeit a shaky one, was created.*
>
> (Royce and Royce, 2008, p 142)

- If families both foster and adopt, and perhaps also have birth children, it is essential to acknowledge the status of each child. Saying that it makes no difference will not make children feel more secure; explaining the reasons for the difference will be much more reassuring.
- Sibling relationships will change as time goes on. Adjustment problems may come later for birth children who initially welcomed

an incoming sibling. Sibling relationships should be regularly reviewed as part of the placement support plan.

Working with siblings-to-be

In their study of long-term sibling placements, Rushton *et al* (2001) found that specialist help with sibling relationships was rare; therapeutic work tended to focus on children and parents separately.

Preparing birth children or established adopted children for the reception of a specific child or sibling group requires skilled direct work. It should not be covered by a one-off interview or a chat when they come home from school. It should involve a planned programme of work with the aims and content agreed and supported by the parents. Some sessions could include all the children as well as their parents, but each child ought to have the opportunity to be heard on his or her own. Birth children are not a "package deal", as one boy said after the family placement worker had seen three children together and assumed that they all shared the positive opinions of the assertive older sister.

There can be no format for this work. Every circumstance will be unique and require individual attention. The lengths and frequency of sessions will vary according to the number, status and ages of the children in the permanent family, the number and ages of the children to be placed, and everyone's previous experiences. Like all direct work with children, it should involve more than talking.

- Family circles are a good way to start: who is in them and how do you open them up to include a newcomer? Will Grandma be their grandma too?
- Why do some children need new families? This can be illustrated by examples from literature or by inviting children to join in storytelling sessions.
- What exactly is adoption and how is it different from fostering? BAAF has published two simple booklets that will help to answer these questions (see *Further reading* at the end of this chapter).
- How can children belong to two families and how can two family trees grow together?
- Making lists of rules children should abide by, deciding which are

important and why, can focus on understanding behaviour and discussing what is acceptable and what is not.

- Naming emotions by drawing faces, and role-plays to practise dealing with situations, will give some idea of children's deeper feelings and of their resilience.

- Many children are concerned about "what to say". What do you tell your friends and your teacher about getting a new brother who is not a baby?

- What is different and what is the same about building a family by adoption? What kind of problems might there be? What do you expect, wish for, fear or pretend? Children can be encouraged to keep an adoption notebook to jot down anything that occurs to them in between direct work sessions.

- How does love grow and will there be enough to go round? Children may believe that their parents' love is finite or be disappointed if they and their new sibling do not instantly love each other. The bucket of love exercise engages most children.

Everyone is born with a bucket full of love. As they are loved and learn to love others, this love is sloshed from one bucket to another, so that all the buckets stay more or less full. But sometimes, when children aren't looked after properly, they spill their love all over the place, and they don't get any back, and then their bucket is nearly empty and they put clingfilm over it so that they won't lose all their love, but the clingfilm doesn't only stop the love from leaking out, it stops love from other buckets getting in.

There are rich opportunities for using this idea to reassure children that their parents' buckets and their own are always full because they give and take love and that there is enough to fill up the new sibling's bucket, but that it may take time to get through the clingfilm.

- Adult children who no longer live at home should not be excluded; on the one hand, they can have strong views about being replaced by a "second family" or about having unwelcome responsibilities foisted upon them, but on the other hand, they may offer an invaluable contribution to making a placement succeed.

If adopters repeatedly tell us that they didn't know how it would really be until they were actually doing it, how could children know? Good support and a forum for children to express their views must follow good preparation. The work with children in prospective permanent families should not be a frill added on to an adoption or fostering package, but an integral part of it. Many disruptions of permanent placements occur because that work has been perfunctory. Clearly, doing it properly is costly and time-consuming, but it should never be a question of 'Can we afford the resources?', but rather, 'Can we afford not to find the resources?'

When people ask if she's my real sister, I say, 'Course she is, 'cause we adopted her together, as a family'.

(Roxy, aged 10)

Further reading

For adults

Astley N (ed) (2002) *Staying Alive: Real poems for unreal times*, London: Bloodaxe

Betts B and Ball R (2005) *Just a Member of the Family* DVD, London: BAAF/B B Media (this film features a number of birth children who have adopted one child or a sibling group.)

Cairns B (2004) *Fostering Attachments*, London: BAAF

Carr K (2007) *Adoption Undone*, London: BAAF

Marsden R (2008) *The Family Business*, London: BAAF

Royce R and Royce E (2008) *Together in Time*, London: BAAF

Rushton A, Dance C, Quinton D and Mayes D (2001) *Siblings in Late Permanent Placements*, London: BAAF

For children

Camis J (2003) *We are Fostering*, London: BAAF

Shah S (2003) *Adoption: What it is and what it means*, London: BAAF

Shah S (2003) *Fostering: What it is and what it means*, London: BAAF

Shah S with Argent H (2006) *Life Story Work: What it is and what it means*, London: BAAF

TIP 8

Support siblings and families after placement

> *Clearly, support that is offered may not be perceived as supportive by the recipient. Indeed, providers of support tend to assume that they are giving more than receivers think they are being given. Just as importantly, support is not static and givers' and receivers' understanding of support may change over time.*
>
> *(O'Neill, 2003, p 9)*

The above quote encapsulates the two essential elements of support: it is as good as it feels, and it has to be flexible enough to meet changing needs. Very few families are completely self-reliant; most depend on some measure of emotional and practical help from friends, neighbours and relatives. All families who adopt or permanently foster should have a built-in support package; families who adopt or foster a sibling group, or who create a new sibling group by adding to their existing children, will probably need support in ratio with the number of their children.

Points to consider

- Every person affected by adoption has a right, according to the 2005 Adoption Support Regulations (England), to have an individual adoption support plan, and that includes any combination of adopted or birth siblings. Scotland, Wales and Northern Ireland already have, or are formulating, similar measures. Good practice would indicate that children who foster and who are permanently fostered, as well as the foster carers, should be given the same kind of attention. Placement support should never be tacked on as an extra at the end of the placement process; discussions about what kind of support may be required, is available, and could be provided, should form an integral part of training, preparation and assessment. 'Come back if you've got a problem' does not constitute a support plan.
- Some children like to talk to someone they can trust outside the family, while others do not. Not every child in a sibling group will have the same communication needs or abilities, or the same needs of any kind, for that matter. Children should be offered one-to-one opportunities as well as group sessions with and without their parents.
- What feels supportive to one family may feel unhelpful, or more like supervision, to another. One adoptive parent with several children may want to unload their problems and recharge their batteries by talking regularly to a skilled counsellor, while another may want expert practical and financial advice.
- However generous the allowances for a sibling group, not all families have the same attitude to money: what seems like plenty to one family may not be enough for another.
- Some permanent carers and some children will like meeting in peer support groups, while others may not. One adopter of two brothers said: 'We've got enough problems of our own without getting upset by other people's'. But nearly all permanent carers and their children appreciate being linked with another family in

similar circumstances.

- Having a support worker from their own ethnic group may be important to some families but not to others. Cultural competence will be important for all. Workers experienced in direct work with children and in working with sibling groups are a necessity rather than a bonus.

- Health and education matters can become very complicated when several children are placed together. Some permanent carers can deal with this, but others may require assistance with forms, procedures and red tape.

- If families have adopted or if they foster several children, they may have to deal with a raft of experts, some coming in and out of their house, especially if any of their children have diagnosed special needs.

> *Maria and Tom fostered and later adopted three unrelated children with a diversity of special needs. They were visited by teachers from their children's schools, by at least three social workers, by a home chiropodist and dentist, by a mobility and welfare rights officer, by a health visitor and by volunteers from a local charity. The family felt inundated by unco-ordinated support. They needed the help they were getting, but Tom said, 'There's a lot of overlap and it's left to us to sort it out, and we don't have any time left just to be a family'.*
>
> (Argent and Coleman, 2006, p 65)

- A post-placement worker might provide effective help by convening an annual meeting of all the professionals involved to listen to the family and to plan a comprehensive joined-up service for the year ahead.

- Short breaks may be essential for all the members of a large family, but they are only supportive if they can be tailored to needs. Some families find it helpful to be able to plan their breaks a year ahead, while others want the chance of respite only if and when they most need it. Not all the children may share the same interests, and it could be beneficial to have a break from each other as well as from parents. However, even short-term separation from parents and from siblings will need careful preparation and monitoring. Children can panic if their exhausted parents leave them to recuperate or if they are taken away from their brothers and sisters.

> *When all three children seemed settled, Maria and Tom, above, went away on their own for the first time for five years, leaving the children at home with a carer provided by their well-meaning local authority. While the parents were away, the children "stole" food, deliberately broke toys and dishes, wet their beds, and generally regressed to earlier behaviours. They had not been enabled to keep their trust in their absent parents in their minds.*
>
> *(Argent and Coleman, 2006, p 65)*

Common issues with sibling groups

The problems that may occur when a number of siblings are placed together or when children are adopted or fostered to create new sibling groups will be as varied as the children themselves, but some issues can be singled out as particularly relevant.

Giving and sharing attention

Parents know how difficult it can be to adjust to what feels like being split in two when a new child is added to the family, and children certainly feel the difference when the "usurper" arrives. There is only a finite amount of attention we can each give, even if we have an infinite amount of love to offer.

A childless farming couple took on a group of four siblings ranging in age from three to eight. No amount of preparation could have brought home the reality of the children's desperate claims for attention. Meals were a constant battle to be heard, bed time and bath time brought escalating tears and temper tantrums, and the farm animals were at risk of torture. If the parents tried to give the children individual attention, the others would disrupt whatever didn't include them; if the group was together, the competition for attention undermined every activity.

Luckily, these parents were totally committed, imaginative and inventive. They devised games to make meals fun and rewarding: games in which everyone round the table had to take it in turn to add to the shopping list, to guess a riddle or to make up a never-ending story in order to qualify for the pudding. Later, meals provided an opportunity to take turns to tell the news of the day. Eventually, each child was able to earn attention by taking responsibility for a task on the farm: collecting eggs, feeding the goat, grooming the pony and tending the orphaned baby lambs. They also learned that they got even more praise and attention if they helped each other out.

One child speaks for all

It can be worrying if only one child in a family is ever heard and the others communicate through their behaviour alone. It can be a simple matter to say: 'OK, I'm glad you told me, now let's see if we can each add a little bit', but it may take more effort to encourage "distant" children to accept attention, and it could then be easier not to notice developing problems. Birth children sometimes feel they have to retreat if their parents seem to be entirely taken up with the newcomers. This is what one adoptive parent wrote about her eight-year-old birth daughter after a younger child was placed with them.

> *The fact is we just assumed Hannah was fine; she appeared to be so undemanding and secure it was easy to overlook her needs. But the hurt to Hannah has been long-lasting, and she still feels that I let her down.*
>
> *(Carr, 2007, p 87)*

The parents do not feel in control

If several children are placed together, it can feel more like a takeover than an adoption. Parent can be left wondering whether their home is still their own and ask themselves: 'Who is in charge?'

> *One of the hardest things for the adoptive father in this situation is the feeling of having absolutely no authority. For years I'd run a business, employed people, supervised contracts, dealt with clients. I wasn't Richard Branson but I managed. I sorted out problems and controlled situations. Here I was, in my mid-forties, totally unable to control a child and my life.*
>
> *(Royce and Royce, 2008, p 17)*

Children who appear to be controlling are usually scared stiff because in fact they really have no control over what happens to them: they have been separated from birth families, moved around foster homes, they have been hurt or neglected; they feel they have been taken apart and they are still looking for someone to put them together again. Giving children a measure of control over their individual day-to-day lives will go some way towards allaying their panic: allowing each child to decide what to wear, to declare preferences about food, to discuss where to go for an outing, to invite their own particular friends to tea, to join in an activity they fancy, like swimming or Scouts or street dancing, will enhance their self-esteem, strengthen their resilience and ultimately enable them to let their parents take charge. Packing the lot of them off to football, wearing the same gear, after sausages for tea for all, may be easier to manage but will not build up their confidence. At the same time, we have to be careful not to give children too many choices. Asking which of five kinds of cereal they would like for breakfast can feel quite threatening to unconfident children; giving a clear choice between cornflakes and rice crispies offers them control over what they eat.

Blaming and shaming

Siblings who have shared a traumatic past may blame each other and their new sisters and brothers for everything from not putting the top on the toothpaste to kicking the dog, even if they were seen to be doing it. "It's not my fault" and "telling tales" is something all very young children try to get away with, but most of them soon come to understand that mistakes can be forgiven, and that taking responsibility for actions is the most acceptable way forward. If children have never been forgiven, and even blamed for what they have not done, then they cannot regulate their own feelings of shame. They will either try to shift all blame onto the others, or one may take the blame for everything their siblings do, and suffer unbearable guilt.

Permanent carers can best deal with this sensitive situation by demonstrating "forgiveness". 'I know how cross you felt when you kicked Pluto, now let's stroke him and show him that you love him and you're sorry you hurt him'. Or, 'It's a pity you broke that plate, but it was an accident and we can go and buy another next time we're out shopping together'. Even a punishment can be made to sound reassuring: 'I'm sorry you won't be able to watch television tonight' will not make a child feel as shamed as: 'No television until you learn to tell the truth'.

Excessive sibling rivalry

Permanent carers often complain that it is not helpful if well-meaning people tell them that the intense rivalry between their children is "normal", when they can clearly see that it is not. If children have come through a difficult past by fighting each other for whatever was going, they are hardly likely to change their way of operating as soon as they are placed in different circumstances. Parents need help to reduce the rivalry, not to tolerate an unlimited amount of it. Giving each child separate attention, like the farming family earlier, will go some way towards that. As the children learn to trust that they will all be kept warm and fed and safe, and that there is enough love to go round, so they will be able to "normalise" their behaviour toward each other – but it can be very hard for parents to witness their struggle and to go on believing that sibling relationships are worth preserving.

Closing ranks and "ganging up"

It can be daunting to be confronted by a row of angry or blank faces, all seeming to accuse the parents of something unfathomable.

> *One single adoptive parent said that she felt like a goalkeeper with five of them playing against her and no one else in her team. This parent slowly changed the game by telling stories. She interwove the children's narratives into her own family stories and together they created new stories and rituals and games in which the players were forever changing sides.*

If birth children are on the home team, they will need a great deal of support from their parents in the early days. It may be advisable for the whole family to participate in family-building exercises guided by a practitioner skilled in creative therapies. It is not wise to loosen the ties too quickly if they have helped the siblings to survive, even if the ties appear to be more like confining chains.

Fairness and equal shares

Parents do not treat all their children exactly the same or feel exactly the same way towards each child. That does not mean that they love or value or nurture some children more than others, but simply that each human relationship is as unique as people are. Parents may have an overall ethic of fairness, but they adjust their actions and reactions to their children's personalities. Permanent carers of sibling groups sometimes feel guilty about this very normal state of affairs, especially if they are constantly challenged by the perennial childhood cry of: 'That's not fair!' Carers need reassurance that they do not have to be the arbitrators of fair shares, but they do have to be able to respond to their children's individual needs and anxieties about "not getting enough".

Birth children can feel unfairly treated if newcomers are allowed to get away with bad behaviour or to have what they regard as special treats.

> *Adeola was jealous and resentful because her new much younger sister, Femi, was allowed to eat chocolate and crisps and to drink Coke – things not usually offered in the household. Explaining that Femi was used to these things, that they would be bad for Adeola, and that Femi would gradually learn to give them up, didn't make Adeola feel any better. But when her parents decided to let Femi introduce these items to the whole family, Adeola was delighted with what she regarded as her new sister's achievement. After the initial settling-in phase, crisps and chocolate and Coke became rare treats, but they did remain on the family menu, and Femi retained the credit.*

Factors influencing sibling relationships in the permanent family

● Timing of entry into the family and siblings' ages and position in the family – who is being displaced?

● Family values – what is important and what is not? In families with many children, it may be necessary to lower some standards but to firmly uphold others.

● Openness – are issues discussed before they become problems? For instance, is inappropriate sexual activity simply ignored or acknowledged and dealt with?

● Attitude to the birth family – are the siblings involved in contact and communication with the birth family in ways that leave no room for splitting and scapegoating?

● The opportunities provided by the family to continue and to build shared sibling experiences.

● How the permanent carers deal with different ethnicities within the family: if only one child is the victim of racism, the sibling relationship may be affected if the parents overcompensate that child.

● Commitment to the whole sibling group and to each member of the sibling group as "special"?

One in, one out

Some of the most difficult childcare decisions are those involving siblings: not only decisions about whether siblings should be placed together, but also decisions about when one child should be removed from a placement and from their sibling group. It can happen that one child remains an outsider – usually the child that was most rejected by the birth family – while the others settle; it may be that one child becomes ill with anxiety about the behaviour of a sibling that threatens the security of the placement for all. When carers have requested that only one child be removed from a placement, Rushton and Dance (2004), in their study of outcomes of late permanent placements, found that prior to an adoption order it was more likely that all the children would return to the care of the local authority, but after an order had been made, there were cases of only one child leaving the family and the sibling group.

> *Faced with the painful task of having to remove one child out of a sibling group, professionals have to assess not only whether these children would do better together or apart, but they will also have to balance the value of a known good placement for one or more against the value of an unknown future for the intact group.*
>
> *(Argent and Coleman, 2006, p 13)*

Not only professionals but also carers agonise about adding further losses to children who have already been so seriously disadvantaged. But the time may come when taking a child out of the sibling group is a necessary step for that child's well-being.

> *About two years ago, I think I nearly had a nervous breakdown. I couldn't stop crying and I realised that no matter what I did, he would never accept me. He tells us, 'You only adopted me because without me you wouldn't have been able to adopt my little brother'.*
>
> *(Adopter quoted in Rushton and Dance, 2004, p 56)*

Just as carers may bond with one child and not another, so one child in a sibling group may refuse to be parented in spite of every effort by family and professionals. Enabling permanent carers to say that they cannot go on has to be part of offering a comprehensive support package, but it is necessary to differentiate between a cry for help and a plea for closure.

> *I told them I couldn't go on – she was killing me and all the kids were suffering. They said they'd take her away if I wanted – they didn't seem to understand – I love that child – I wasn't asking for her to go – but I couldn't cope without them doing something.*
>
> (Permanent foster carer of three siblings)

Further reading

Argent H and Coleman J (2006) *Dealing with Disruption*, London: BAAF

Carr K (2007) *Adoption Undone*, London: BAAF

O'Neill C (2003) 'The simplicity and complexity of support' in Argent H (ed) *Models of Adoption Support*, London: BAAF

Post-adoption Centre (2008) *Supporting Black and Minority Ethnic Children*, training pack, Section one: Siblings, London: Post-adoption Centre

Royce R and Royce E (2008) *Together in Time*, London: BAAF

Rushton A and Dance C (2004) 'The outcomes of late permanent placements: the adolescent years', *Adoption & Fostering*, 28:1, pp 49–58

TIP 9

Ensure that parted siblings can share their lives

This nostalgia of theirs is extraordinary, each of them feels the richness of it. On and on they'll talk; a whole afternoon will disappear while they take turns comparing and repeating their separate and shared memories and shivering with pleasure every time a fresh segment is unearthed. Memory could be poked with a stick, and savoured in the mouth like a popsicle, you could never get enough of it.

(Shields, 1995, p 175)

Children who have shared painful events may not delight in all their memories like the siblings above, but it may be even more urgent for them to bear witness to each other's experiences. If the aim of contact between parted siblings is focused on enabling them to continue to share their lives, then the other desirable elements of "keeping in touch" will automatically be included.

- Maintaining, restoring and building life-long relationships
- Putting the pieces of fragmented lives together
- Dealing with reality rather than fantasy
- Minimising the trauma of loss and separation
- Confirming identity
- Preserving continuity

Good contact arrangements for siblings will have more to do with quality than quantity: the frequency of visits and where they take place has to be determined, to some extent, by practical matters such as distance and available time; how they are managed will depend on the attitudes of the care-taking families and their personal and professional support networks. Talking freely about absent sisters and brothers and including them in the family circle will lead to communicative openness, enjoyable contact and flexibility; adhering strictly to the letter of a contact agreement and excluding siblings from the family dialogue will result in merely structural openness and in inhibiting sibling interaction (Brodzinsky, 2005). It will lead nowhere except to finding reasons to curtail or terminate contact altogether.

The optimum factors for creating communicative openness are:

- permanent carers of split siblings see positives in preserving continuity for the sibling group;
- birth parents have been included in the decisions and wish their children to remain connected to each other;
- the children hear the same stories from, and are supported in contact arrangements by, all the adults involved;
- the "other" siblings are liked and regarded as extended family by the permanent carers;
- the sets of parents can provide a model for co-operation.

What is needed to maintain continuity will change as circumstances change and as children get older: a three-year-old cannot remember people she doesn't see regularly, but a 10-year-old can keep people in mind; some children feel at ease with the telephone, emails and texting, while others will need face-to-face meetings to make sense of relationships. Formal, mediated letterbox contact for siblings should only be considered if, after full assessments, it is judged unsafe for any other kind of contact to take place. And we have to remember that safety should not mean severance.

Separate placements

If siblings must be separated, it is as well to wait until families have been found before deciding on contact arrangements. Stipulations like "will need to have contact with his brothers four times a year" are off-putting for prospective carers who do not yet know the children. Involving the carers in negotiating arrangements to meet all the children's needs, including contact, can be a valuable part of preparation.

Whatever is envisaged at the permanency planning stage should be open to further discussion with the children, the birth parents and the permanent carers before placements are finalised. If the purpose of staying connected can be agreed, the arrangements should follow more easily; if they do not, it may be helpful to use a mediation service to enable everyone to speak and to be heard without fear of being constrained or put down. It is vital that contact plans are not left vague; vague is no substitute for flexible. Rushton *et al* (2001) found that although new families were broadly committed to maintaining contact with siblings, half of the placements were made without any specific contact plans, and practical problems were not addressed by active social work intervention.

In a study focusing on the views of older adopted children, Thomas and Beckford (1999) found that nearly all separated siblings wished for more contact. When asked how much more, Paul, aged 12, said: 'At least twice a week. Well, twice every two weeks or something like that. Maybe twice a week' (p 102).

Points to consider

- Clear lines of communication between families and professionals: who will manage contact? How will it be arranged? Will all the siblings meet each time or will they also get together in pairs? Some families prefer to make a written contract, while others are more comfortable with flexible plans; some can work together without outside support while others would rather that social workers took responsibility.

- Whole-day activities suit most children better than more formal visits. But days out with several children can be very expensive. One rather well-off adoptive family always wanted to spend the day in a theme park; the other family didn't like to admit that they couldn't afford it, so found reasons to cancel the contact instead. Expenses for contact could have been included in the post-placement plan, and then it might have been possible to agree on a theme park in the summer holidays and more modest outings to cheaper venues for the rest of the year.

- Acknowledgement of ethnic, cultural and socio-economic family lifestyles will ease the contact arrangements. Not only disposable incomes will differ. How families dress, their religious rituals, where they live, what they eat, when they have to work, how they welcome visitors or regard relatives, will all affect how they keep in touch.

A large sibling group was split between two Muslim families: one family was strictly observant; the other had a relaxed view of religion and was keen to assimilate. The two families disapproved of each other's way of bringing up children and contact rapidly withered away.

- Siblings who have been separated for good reasons are likely to have troubled relationships. If they can't live together, they will probably not be able to have positive contact experiences without ongoing therapeutic support.

Joe loved his brothers, and I think that love was reciprocated. The brotherly bond will always exist but there was no working relationship. Their early

> *life had created negative patterns of interaction that hadn't changed. It was frustrating to think there was nothing we could do about it, but all the brothers would need therapy to change the patterns, and that wasn't going to happen. We had to accept it and get on with what we could to improve life for Joe.*
>
> (Royce and Royce, 2008, p 88)

- If children have been sexually abused, and more especially if they have abused each other, contact may reactivate past trauma and should be closely supervised. The purpose of supervision and the role of the supervisor (whether family or professional) have to be clearly defined. Sometimes a birth parent can try to control one sibling through another, or one sibling may put pressure on another to retract or deny the abuse in order to stay in touch.
- Siblings and families need guidelines to understand what information can be freely exchanged and what, if anything, should be kept private for safety reasons, and those reasons should be made explicit. It is not uncommon for contact to be severed between separately placed siblings because one is fostered and in touch with a birth parent, which is automatically considered to endanger the anonymity of a sister's adoptive home. Children cannot, and should not, be relied upon to keep secrets, but successful efforts can be made to involve them in the bigger picture.

> *Twelve-year-old Chanelle, who was fostered, did not disclose her younger sister's adoptive details to her mother until the adoptive family felt secure enough to be open about their identity and location. Chanelle was encouraged to feel that she was playing an important part in keeping her little sister*

> *safe; she loved her visits to the adoptive family and would not have deliberately put her relationship with her sister in jeopardy.*

- Birth children should not be left out of sibling contact, but they may need a bit of extra attention from their parents if they feel temporarily excluded from a special relationship.

> *The second Lucy and Jade saw each other, they just smiled and held each other's gaze, slowly approaching one another for a hug...We watched Hannah trying hard to join in. Jade would try to encourage her, but Hannah only wanted to be close to Lucy. She felt, and was, rejected by her. Lucy was just four years old at the time and it was natural for her to rejoice in the affections of her forcibly estranged sister. From the second Lucy saw Jade, her whole attention was on her.*
>
> *(Carr, 2007, pp 50–51)*

- Grandparents and other relatives are often very good at making a contact day go well because they are not quite as closely involved. Children will probably enjoy parading their new relations, but some work may have to be done to prevent siblings feeling that it's a competition for "best family".
- Regular reviews of expectations met and unmet can explore further what is working well and what might need to be changed. Is any one child feeling left out? What can be done to help the children deal with a renewed sense of loss after meetings? How can they remain more firmly connected between meetings? In an ideal world there would be a named social worker, readily available to all concerned, who has an overview of the sibling relationships and all their placements.

Contact with siblings "at home"

It must be almost unbearable to know that your birth mother has had another baby, but that you are not going to be allowed to see it because you've now got a family of your own, and so on. It could be equally devastating to find out later that children were born after you were removed from the family home whom you knew nothing about, and who most probably know nothing about you.

If there is face-to-face contact with birth parents, there should be no problem about including new infants, or other children who have remained at home, in the arrangements. Specially designated contact centres can generally offer the most suitable venues and support.

If there is only letterbox contact, the "at home" children and the adopted or fostered children can be helped to participate in sending letters, photos, and drawings and to keep them in special sisters and brothers folders. Even absent siblings can be kept in mind and can grow up in the imagination, so that the unseen baby won't always stay a baby. Unless there are quite exceptional circumstances, there should be no excuse for losing siblings altogether.

Having brothers and sisters still living with their birth mother does, of course, raise other issues for the separated siblings. 'Why not us?', or, if there has been serious abuse, 'If we were hurt, the baby might also be hurt' and 'If she couldn't look after us, how will she look after the others?' Contact with "at home" siblings can be both reassuring and troubling; all the children should be prepared for meetings and have the opportunity to talk about it afterwards. Arrangements may or may not include the birth parents, and they should be supervised if there is a risk of "mixed messages".

Contact with foster siblings

This aspect of sibling relationships is sadly overlooked and under-prized. Children who foster may make significant connections with children who move on to be adopted or to permanent foster homes. The feelings of loss on both sides are rarely taken into account.

Theo cried every night when he came to us because he could not understand why the foster carers' young son could not come and live with us as well. We tried to explain that he had his own mummy and daddy, but Theo pointed out that as he had two sets of parents, why couldn't his foster brother? If only we'd had some contact with the foster family in those early days, we could have kept the relationship going for Theo, but we were told it would upset him too much, so we just tried to get him over it. Now we feel he's lost his only brother, because by the time we saw them again, he'd kind of buried his feelings.

(Adopter of four-year-old boy)

Different and changing contact needs

Not all the children in a sibling group will want to have the same contact arrangements with their parents or with each other if they are separated. It is not a "fits one, fits all" programme. Sisters and brothers may not have the same mother or the same father, or they may be at quite different stages in their development: younger children may be very reliant on their siblings while teenagers could be more interested in their peers.

Unrelated adopted or fostered siblings will certainly have individual arrangements, and it can be hard on one to have no contact with their birth family if others are in touch with their birth parents and perhaps also some birth brothers and sisters. As in all family situations, openness is the best policy. Why one child cannot have contact might helpfully become the concern of all, and that child might be happily included in the contact arrangements of the other siblings.

There is only one golden rule about sibling contact: we must keep all arrangements under review because childhood is the time of greatest change and contact needs are one of many changing needs of the developing young person.

I used to go and play with him. I used to go and stay with him for a day and he used to come around to mine sometimes. But we don't do that anymore because he's 15.

(Sophie, aged 12, quoted in Thomas and Beckford, 1999, p 83)

Further reading

Beckett S (2002) 'Split up but not cut off: making and sustaining contact arrangements between siblings', in Argent H, *Staying Connected*, London: BAAF

Brodzinsky D M (2005) 'Reconceptualising openness in adoption: implications for research and practice', in Brodzinsky D M and Palacios J (eds) *Psychological Issues in Adoption: Research and practice*, Westport CT: Praeger

Carr K (2007) *Adoption Undone*, London: BAAF

Macaskill C (2002) *Safe Contact? Children in permanent placements and contact with their birth families*, Lyme Regis: Russell House Publishing

Royce R and Royce E (2008) *Together in Time*, London: BAAF

Rushton A, Dance C, Quinton D and Mayes D (2001) *Siblings in Late Permanent Placements*, London: BAAF

Shields C (1995) *The Stone Diaries*, London: Fourth Estate

Thomas C and Beckford V with Lowe N and Murch M (1999) *Adopted Children Speaking*, London: BAAF

TIP 10

Mark the difference: a checklist for working with siblings

> **Brother should not war with brother**
> **And worry and devour each other**
>
> (The Nightingale and Glow-worm
> William Cowper, 1731–1800)

Working with siblings is not the same as working with more than one child: it is like working with several children from two different directions at the same time. There is the sibling group of which each child is a member, and there is each individual child. The group has a character and momentum of its own and every child has specific attributes and needs. This checklist offers a summary of the key points to keep in mind when working with the children in a sibling group and with their families.

- Sibling groups may be made up of full or half genetically related children, of unrelated fostered children, adopted children or stepchildren, or of mixed birth, fostered and adopted children.
- The aim in direct work with all sibling groups and in every family placement is to make each child special, not equal.
- The presumption should be that siblings will stay together unless it is not safe for them to do so because they would suffer emotional or physical harm; too many children for one family, or having different needs, are not good enough reasons, on their own, to separate brothers and sisters.
- We owe it to siblings to try to heal their damaged relationships, not merely to assess them.
- Children must be helped to understand why they are being separated and the reasons must be recorded.
- Siblings, like all children who cannot stay with their parents, should remain in their families if a relative or friend can care for them. Kinship carers need to be given the resources to make that possible.
- Preparing and working with every kind of existing and potential sibling group, as well as individually with all the children in it, is an essential part of family placement work.
- Each child in a sibling group will have had different personal experiences and developed different attachment styles. One child may be more damaged than the others and have greater difficulty forming bonds with new parents.
- Children may transfer their sibling relationship patterns to the new family's established children, or they may not be able to relate to them until they have learned to trust their new parents.
- Sisters and brothers who have been separated and are reunited will bring the influence of different family systems into the sibling group.
- The roles siblings play in the group and the pecking order can only change after they have made secure attachments to permanent carers.

- Taking responsibility for siblings is seen in some cultures as the appropriate basis for life-long reciprocal relationships rather than as substitute parenting.

- If sibling groups include children of different ethnicities, it is more important to find one family that can celebrate diversity than to split the children up in order to find a perfect match for all.

- A disabled child should not be placed apart from his siblings only because he has special needs; his sisters and brothers have special needs too.

- Children who have had to fight to survive are likely to fight each other for what they can get. This does not mean that they should be separated – it means that they have to get used to being given enough.

- Prospective permanent carers have to claim each child as well as the sibling group. It may aid the attachment process to introduce one child at a time into the new family.

- It is tough for new parents to accept that the children in a sibling group have spent time together and shared experiences from which they must remain excluded.

- It is exhausting to adopt or foster siblings; permanent carers will require high tolerance of noise, mess and disruption of normal activities. They will need stamina for endless shopping and washing and cooking. They would do well to prepare a network of willing helpers.

- Very few people have the resources to take several children, all at once, into their family without substantial support of all kinds, including financial support. It is enough to become parents to a sibling group, without having to worry about money.

- Permanent carers of sibling groups have to be able to devise mechanisms for looking after their own well-being.

- It is not safe to assume that adopted children and birth children close in age will make a viable sibling group; wanting a companion for an only child is not a good reason for adopting or fostering.

- Not all the children in a sibling group will have the same relationships with other members of their birth family, or the same contact needs.

- Openness in bringing up a sibling group of children will avoid fantasies of preferment, rejection, victimisation and hidden agendas.

- It is always essential to work with the birth family in order to make lasting placements. When several children are involved, the birth family will hold the clues to the sibling relationships as well as to each child's history.

> *Our relationships with our siblings are the longest lasting of our lives, longer than those with our partners (even if we stay with the same person), outliving those with parents (assuming a normal life span for all parties), and predating those with our children. If we are lucky, surviving into old age and remaining in touch with our families, our sibling relationships traverse all the traumas not only of childhood but of adulthood too.*
>
> *(Mullender, 1999, p 14)*

Further reading

Mullender A (ed) (1999) *We are Family: Sibling relationships in placement and beyond*, London: BAAF

Endpiece

(The following text has been reproduced with kind permission from *Fostering Attachments*, by Brian Cairns (2004) London: BAAF)

My name is Sarah (or Sal depending whether this is a professional meeting or a private encounter). I am a Probation Officer. I live with my partner of 10 years, Simon, and two cats. I am one of 15 children, 10 boys and five girls. I'm white, middle class and British (or possibly European). My politics sit left of centre although I am able to accept that market economics is here to stay. I was brought up as a Quaker and Quaker teachings continue to offer guidance in my daily life. I could go on.

The bit I'm most often asked to expand on is the 'I'm one of 15 children'. The questions I face include:

Half brothers and sisters?
Are your parents Catholic?
Are your parents mad?

I often find the questions difficult to answer. When I say that some of my brothers and sisters are fostered I am left feeling that judgements have been made. It's almost as if people think, 'Oh, well! That doesn't count'. Assumptions are made that my relationship with my genetic brothers is bound to be different from my relationship with the others and that our relationship with our parents is bound to be different.

The message I would wish to convey is that all 15 of us have a different experience of our relationship with Kate and Brian (parents) and that is about us being individuals. For myself, being born to them is just part of my history, just as having had a choice of five last names when he joined the family was part of Dan's history. In other words, it is important to my identity that my family is viewed as as valid and "real" as the next.

I have often wondered what it is like to be one of my foster siblings explaining to a third party that they are a member of our family. On occasions when the number of siblings has been queried, I have tried to be vague about whether or not I was one of the homegrowns. For example, I will say, 'Some of us are fostered'. However, this inevitably leads to the question, 'Were you?' Clearly the question of genetic origins is important in our society. Having said this, I only started having to offer explanations once I left home. In our home town the family was just accepted.

I was always aware as a child that we were from a number of different ethnic backgrounds. Looking back, I'm surprised that the obvious differences such as skin colour did not raise questions from our peers at school. My experience as a child and something that has been taken into adulthood was accepting ethnicity as just one factor that creates diversity and that diversity is something to be embraced and cherished.

Family and social relationships

I have already described how I do not differentiate between my foster and natural siblings. However, it is important to note that coming from a large family means inevitably that some relationships are closer than others. Of my siblings there are four or five with whom I am in regular contact and whom I'm likely to see outside of my visits home or big family gatherings. It is the case that my two "natural" brothers fall into this group. We do have a lot of shared interests and it is easy to speculate that there may be some additional genetic bond between us that is not present in my other relationships. I don't know if this is the case and on one level I don't really care. Providing that my current closeness to Tom and Rich does not exist at the expense of other relationships, then that is fine.

The important thing here is that at no time have Tom, Rich and I ever thought of ourselves as a subset within the family. At no time have we ever pursued the three of us having a shared relationship to the exclusion of our other siblings. My relationship with Richard is separate from my relationship with Tom, just as it is separate from my relationship with Liam and so on.

For several years, us three birth children held the position as youngest in the family and there was a four year age gap between me and Dan, the youngest of our fostered siblings. Then Kwesi was added to the younger end, and Karen and then Pete came between me and Dan. Finally Liam was added in the middle! I think now if Mum and Dad had left it that all their foster children were going to be four years older or more, our sense of identity may well have developed along "them and us" lines. As it was, the impact of having siblings close in age was experienced on an individual basis. There was no sense of having a private clique intruded upon. However, it was these relationships that were experienced on the most intense level and which, in my view, set our experiences of childhood apart from that of our peers who did not grow up in a foster family.

For me, Karen's arrival in the family had greatest impact. Karen is 10 months older than me and I am almost exactly the same age as her "natural" sister to whom she was very close. I can remember being very excited prior to Karen's arrival about having a new sister, and one so close in age to me. However, things did not work out quite as I had envisaged. Over the next three years our relationship was characterised by short periods of being very close to longer periods of hating each other. We can both look back now and analyse the processes that were being played out. We now laugh about the time that Karen punched me full in the face and then ran off into the hills surrounding Stroud, disappearing for a worrying six hours (about the same amount of time as it took for my nose to stop bleeding!).

Throughout my childhood I always enjoyed having a number of close friendships and I rarely suffered bullying. But there were, I now realise, ways in which being part of a foster family impacted on my social relationships. I remember when I was about six or seven inviting a school friend to tea. As we all sat down at the table to eat, my friend burst into tears, completely overwhelmed by the whole experience. It was the only time I was allowed to take my tea (and my friend) to eat in front of the television. That friend never came to tea again. Unlike my friends, I tended to shy away from having birthday parties, choosing instead to have a birthday treat with maybe just one or two of my closest friends.

Emotional and behavioural development

I would expect that my emotional and behavioural development as a child would have been viewed by my teachers and any social worker who might have wanted to observe as "normal". I laughed, played and cried as a young child, I developed an interest in how I looked and in boys as a teenager, I became stroppy and uncommunicative with my mum for a few months when I was about 13, I rebelled a bit when I was 15, 16, 17 by smoking and bouts of underage drinking, and when I left home and went to university I smoked cannabis. These are phases I was likely to have gone through whether or not I had foster brothers and sisters. However, there were some aspects of my development that were directly linked to my experience of being a birth child in a foster family.

Members of the family often describe me as the "peacemaker". I don't think this is an entirely accurate description, as trying "to come in between" or to sort out disputes was not something I particularly did. However, I did from a young age concern myself with family affairs. An early memory (I must have been eight or nine) was of listening to Mum and Dad at the pantry hatch having a "discussion" with John. In other words, John was in trouble! For some reason I felt I needed to know what was going on so that I could do everything possible to either help make things right or stop things getting worse. By "things" I think I mean the smooth and harmonious running of the household. I remember on later occasions realising, often together with Dan, that things were not necessarily calm on the western front, and deciding it would be a good idea to lay the table or hang the washing out or do something that would take some pressure off Mum and Dad.

As I got older, I found myself almost appointing myself as a "deputy parent" to my younger brothers (Tom, Liam, Rich and Kwesi). I was in some ways the archetypal bossy older sister, but I actually think this ran deeper. When Mum and Dad found their inner resources increasingly stretched as a result of cutbacks and the unavailability of adequate professional support, I took on a greater level of responsibility towards my younger siblings, ranging from the practical – cooking, shopping, cleaning – to the more emotional – trying to advise and offer guidance. I think this was not comparable to the experience of my peers, but I do not think it was in any way harmful to me. I believe it actually enhanced my emotional and behavioural development, and I consider that if there had been any hint of the growing responsibilities I took on within the family being too much for me, Mum and Dad would have intervened.

Another element of emotional and behavioural development is the expectation that birth children will cope. We will not go off the rails and we will succeed in most aspects of our lives. I'm not saying that Mum and Dad placed this expectation on us, but we were aware from quite a young age of the links between early childhood trauma and subsequent problems. This awareness enabled us to understand the sometimes difficult and stressful behaviour of some of our siblings, and in understanding we were able to help them through recovery. Such understanding, however, meant for me that being "good" was a conscious process. It also meant that in my self-appointed role as deputy parent, my chastening of Tom and Rich was more severe than of Kwesi or Liam.

It is difficult to be objective about being a birth child in a foster family because it's about being me. I'm the subject. I guess the message is that any child has only one shot at childhood and the decisions their parents or carers make determine what that is going to be like. For me, my mum and dad did an alright job! I'm one of 15, I can't change that, and frankly I wouldn't want to because that would be to change me!

Sally Poskett

Useful organisations

British Association for Adoption and Fostering (BAAF)
Head Office
Saffron House
6–10 Kirby Street
London
EC1N 8TS
Tel: 020 7421 2600
www.baaf.org.uk

BAAF Cymru
7 Cleeve House
Lambourne Crescent
Cardiff
CF14 5GP
Tel: 029 2076 1155

BAAF Scotland
40 Shandwick Place
Edinburgh
EH2 4RT
Tel: 0131 220 4749

BAAF Northern Ireland
Botanic House
1–5 Botanic Avenue
Belfast
BT7 1JG
Tel: 028 9031 5494

Adoption UK
46 The Green
South Bar Street
Banbury
OX16 9AB
Tel: 01295 752240
www.adoptionuk.org

Adults Affected by Adoption – NORCAP
112 Church Road
Wheatley
Oxfordshire
OX33 1LU
Tel: 01865 875000
www.norcap.org.uk

Family Rights Group
Second Floor
The Print House
18 Ashwin Street
London E8 3DL
Tel: 020 7923 2628
www.frg.org.uk

Fostering Network
87 Blackfriars Road
London
SE1 8HA
Tel: 020 7620 6400
www.fostering.net

The Grandparents' Association
Moot House
The Stow
Harlow
Essex
CM20 3AG
Tel: 01279 428040
www.grandparents-association.org.uk

Grandparents Plus
18 Victoria Park Square
Bethnal Green
London E2 9PF
Tel: 020 8981 8001
www.grandparentsplus.org.uk

Siblings United
Shaftesbury Young People
The Chapel, RVPB
Trinity Road
London SW18 3SX
Tel: 020 8875 1555
www.shaftesbury.org.uk
Organises "summer camps" together for siblings separated in care.